Beyond Survival

A Holocaust Memoir

Kenneth Arkwright

16pt

Copyright Page from the Original Book

Published by Hybrid Publishers

Melbourne Victoria Australia

First published 2018

A catalogue record for this book is available from the National Library of Australia

Cover design by Art on Order
Typeset in Minion Pro
Printed in Australia by McPherson's Printing Group

All photographs and documents courtesy of the author Ken Arkwright unless otherwise indicated.

TABLE OF CONTENTS

Introduction	ii
The Beginning	1
Smells	8
My Heroes	16
Boycott	28
Gathering of the Storm	46
The Inferno	69
The Closed Door	97
Going Nowhere	112
The Plot Thickens	123
The Unfolding of the Plan	139
Watching and Waiting	156
Moving On	167
The Camps	184
Christmas Trees	197
Loam and Vinegar	207
Schwanzparade	220
Loewenstein	227
Holy Water	233
The Canoe	240
The End of the Beginning	250
Halka	257
Porta Coeli	266
The Girl with One Leg	281
Hebrew Lessons	293
The Princess	302
The Dog	311
Terra Australis	318
Unity or Diversity?	325

"The world is a tragedy to those who feel, but a comedy to those who think." – Horace Walpole (1717-97)

Introduction

I am a Jew. Between 1933 and 1945 I lived in Germany, the country of my birth, with the many who perished and with the few who survived the Holocaust.

It did not occur to me at that time, that one day the daily battle for survival would lead me towards the inevitable end of my life. As every day passes, there is more of the past to remember and less of the future to anticipate.

I have learnt that life is a journey. Its fulfilment cannot be found in some high place on the way, but in having made this journey from childhood to old age.

I have no regrets, harbour no hate, claim no privilege, but I feel a deep gratitude for every single moment of my life and for every human encounter along the way.

My friends and my enemies, the light of day, and the hours of darkness, have guided me along this path. To them I owe the knowledge that the purpose of life cannot be found beyond survival, but in sharing the lessons learnt along this road with my fellow travellers.

Many years of reflecting on these events had to take place to make me feel the need to write about this journey. May the world of yesterday give courage and hope to all who are building the world of tomorrow!

Ken Arkwright during an interview about the Holocaust in a series of interviews: "Sprechen trotz allem – Voices of Survival". Photo: Stiftung Denkmal für die ermordeten Juden Europas

1

The Beginning

> "Life is like riding a bicycle. To keep your balance, you must keep moving." – Albert Einstein (1879-1955)

I arrived in this world in the (then) German city of Breslau on Tuesday, 16 April 1929, at 1.45am. I must already have been swollen-headed, as Ms Weinhausen, my mother's midwife, had difficulties in helping me progress from the relative safety of my mother's womb into a world that was rapidly sliding into economic depression, mass unemployment and political extremism.

Ms Weinhausen had to enlist the assistance of Dr Lili Berg-Platau, my mother's obstetrician. Dr Berg-Platau was a friend of our family. She left Germany shortly after my arrival to live in Palestine. She and her family were committed Zionists, a world view that was considered misguided by most of our family and friends. At that time, we felt completely at home in our German fatherland.

Lili's close friends at the Breslau Friedrich Wilhelm University were Erna and Edith Stein. Erna Stein acquired Lili's medical practice after Lili had emigrated to Palestine. Edith Stein left Judaism and became a nun, which did not save her from being gassed in Auschwitz. The Catholic Church did little to highlight Hitler's crimes in the world, other than making Edith Stein a saint called "St Teresa Benedicta of the Cross".

On Tuesday, 23 April 1929, at 10.30am, Dr Schlesinger introduced me into the "Covenant of Abraham" through the rite of circumcision. I was told that it was a great occasion for our family. To be frank, I cannot remember a thing about it! My father's cousins, Alfred Redlich and Fritz Ritter, were my godfathers. Who could have guessed at that time that Alfred, his wife Käthe and their son Walter would be deported to Kaunas-Lithuania on 25 November 1941. There the 693 men, 1,155 women and 152 children of this transport had to dig their graves and then were shot on 29 November, a mere 72 hours after leaving Breslau. Fritz Ritter died in

Breslau, but his wife Elli Ritter was gassed in Auschwitz in 1944.

Alfred, Käthe (16) and Walter Redlich (9).

The first four years of my` life were perfectly normal and happy, although they coincided with the dying years of the Weimar Republic. Democratic Germany was fighting a losing battle against its most serious opponent, the National Socialist German Workers Party led by Adolf Hitler.

Two months after my birth, my mother returned to work in my father's business. My grandparents supervised my upbringing and showered me with great love and affection. Occasional corrective action by my parents was required. The polarity between the gentleness of my grandparents and the disciplinarian approach of my parents did not cause any confusion in my mind. It was perceived by me as two different manifestations of loving care and attention.

Life started in earnest after my third birthday. On 1 October 1932 I joined a small private Montessori kindergarten, located in a palatial apartment building, in Kaiser Wilhelm Strasse. It was managed by Dr Käthe (Catherine) Stern (1894-1973), a scientist who later became a researcher in children's education. Being of Jewish origin, she had to emigrate in 1938 to the USA.

In kindergarten we were given the opportunity to select one toy at a time, and were not allowed to exchange this toy for another for one long hour. We had to abandon the toy after the hour had elapsed. Every one of us had our own pot plant to care for. The twenty plants stood side by side on a flower bench with our name tag attached to it. There was no replacement for plants that had died through neglect. A flowerpot containing a dead plant standing next to another that flourished, told the story. No further praise or chastisement was required. We had to observe a quiet hour during which no one was allowed to speak.

Only one piece of paper and coloured pencils were given to each child. This made us think before putting marks on the paper. All this was designed to make us thoughtful, considerate, and to appreciate an orderly world. The daily reports about my conduct still exist, and they gave me an insight into the formation of my thought processes and attitudes.

Every afternoon my nanny, Lotte Abraham, a trained kindergarten teacher, played with me and took me for outings to the nearby Kaiser Wilhelm Platz. The one-to-one relationship with Lotte, in contrast to the group environment in the kindergarten, made me appreciate the uniqueness and kindness of every human soul. I revisited Breslau (which reverted to Poland after the war and was renamed Wrocław) in 1997 and found the Kaiser Wilhelm Platz had changed its name to Plac Powstańców Śląskich. The sand patch in which Lotte played with me is still there, but her life was terminated in the gas chambers of Auschwitz.

My three kindergarten years (1932-35) introduced me to a world worth striving for, and they also taught me to distinguish between right and wrong. Meanwhile, however, the real world around me was moving in the opposite direction.

My favourite ice-cream shop had a sign on its entrance door, *Juden unerwünscht* (Jews not wanted). Park benches were stencilled "Not for Jews". These signs disappeared for the month of August 1936, during the Olympic Games in Germany. The man selling balloons, toys and ice-cream on the Kaiser Wilhelm Platz would no longer deal with Jews.

My father's business became *arisiert* (Aryanised). He was ordered to do forced labour, building autobahns in Werlte, near Hannover. The real world and the world as it could have been, became increasingly difficult to reconcile.

We were not only German-Jews by name, but we had our roots in both German and Jewish culture. Hitler's policies made us explore and consider the true nature of our identity. It has remained for me an ongoing task to reconcile the ideal world, that was created in my mind at an early age, and the real world in which my life takes place.

The often maligned and misquoted German philosopher, Friedrich Nietzsche, defines the Jewish identity problem succinctly in his book *The Dawn of Day:* "In Europe, they [the Jews] have gone through a schooling of eighteen centuries such as no other nation has ever undergone, and the experiences of this dreadful time of trials have benefited not only the Jewish community but, even to a greater extent, the individual."

Smells

> "Life is the childhood of our immortality." – Johann Wolfgang von Goethe (1749-1832)

Historians are expected to present data in an orderly fashion. They sort events into a logical sequence of time and place. However, this is not the Jewish way to write history. To Jews, history is not merely a systematic record of the past; it is the lesson of the past for the future. Thomas Carlyle once wrote: "Jews are a people without history". He failed to see that to the Jews, history is the response of man to the world and to his fellow men.

I have told you a little about those who came before me, and who brought about the beginning of my journey through life. What follows are glimpses of what I have seen and experienced on this journey, how I remember it, and how it helped to make me what I am today. When one tries to remember events of early childhood, reality and stories told about these years by family and friends merge. There is little merit in trying to separate the immediate personal experience of my life from the stories about my life, as told to me by others. History and story have merged and have become the reality of my life.

In January 1933, we lived in a beautiful part of Breslau (Charlottenstrasse 8) in a fifteen-room apartment. Most of the furniture was made especially for this apartment and in addition it was furnished with many exquisite antique pieces. The "Big Living Room" had to be heated by two beautiful tiled stoves and these stoves had to be fired a week in advance to make the room comfortable and cosy for the twenty-five or more visitors who attended frequent dinner parties. The live-in maid, Maria, donned a special black dress, a white serving apron and a white bonnet to attend to the guests at the table and to help them into their overcoats when they were leaving.

The Persian floor rugs, windows treated with kilims, hand-embroidered curtains and beautiful paintings gave the apartment a most elegant appearance. It required a large staff to maintain our home and I remember many of them with great affection.

Every morning, the first caller was Frau Wahl. She set my grandmother's hair with curling shears, which she heated over a methylated spirit flame. She tested the temperature of the shears on pieces of newspaper before applying them to my grandmother's hair. The smell of the singed paper and of the methylated spirit flame still lingers on. She was not merely a servant, but a friend. In addition, she was the "Newspaper of the Jewish community of Breslau", spreading the latest gossip from home to home.

The French polisher came once a year to restore all furniture, and once a month the caretaker took all the Persian rugs into the yard to beat the dust out of them. Maria attended to the general cleaning. Every two months Frau Müssigbrot came to do the "big wash" and she was followed by Klara, the mending lady.

At lunchtime, Leo, the business-lift-driver, collected my parents' midday meal from our home to deliver this meal to my parents in their business. All businesses in the city were closed between one and two for a meal break and they then traded until 7pm. Leo, although not Jewish, looked like one of the caricatures of Jews in the anti-Semitic newspaper, the *Stürmer.* He had a large family to feed, an alcohol problem to deal with and a hunchback to contend with. My parents tried to help his family and they always left parcels of extra food and any surplus clothing for him.

Every one of these servants were friends and they always had a kind word to say to me. Every one of them created a distinctive, unforgotten scent which conjures up my recollection of them all.

The smouldering newspaper; the French polish; the smell of soap suds from the laundry; the Christmas tree in the maids' room, which I was allowed to look at, but which had no other place in our apartment, and finally the smell of dinners that escaped from the food carrier collected by Leo.

Most Sunday mornings, a horse-drawn cab was hired to take us to the Terrace Restaurant in the

Scheitniger Park for breakfast. An orchestra entertained the breakfast guests, and I, as well as many other children, stood behind the conductor, copying his conducting activity. On the way home, we visited members of our large family. Maria had midday dinner ready when we returned home. In the afternoon, friends of my parents and grandparents came to visit for coffee and a chat. I was dressed for the occasion to meet them. Thereafter, my nanny Lottel would take me out to play. Later in the early evening I was put to bed while my parents went to the opera, the theatre, concerts, or visited their close friends. Occasionally members of our family from other parts of Germany visited and stayed with us.

I vaguely remember some of the more colourful visitors. There was my grandfather's good friend, Arnold Karfunkelstein, who had a villa in the Breslau suburb of Scheitnig with a large garden in which he kept exotic animals that he had brought home from his travels to Africa. Arnold also had Germany's most comprehensive stamp collection, confiscated after 1933 by the

Nazis. My grandfather's cousin, Paul Aufrichtig, worked in a firm of antique dealers and interior decorators, specialising in furnishing castles and manor houses.

The Gnadenfelds had a luxury leather goods business which was a landmark in Gartenstrasse, Breslau's top shopping district. I met Mr Gnadenfeld again after the war in the Jewish Aged Home in Berlin. He had survived the Theresienstadt concentration camp. To be more precise, his body had survived, but his mind was gone and there was nothing left we could talk about.

And then there were the Silbermanns with their "deaf and dumb" son Erich. I always dreaded their visit, as Erich wanted to be nice to me but I found him extremely hard to understand. Rabbi Dr Jacob Sänger often called to discuss B'nai Brith business. While life in our elegant and luxurious surroundings was relatively free from economic worries, there were many members of the Breslau Jewish community living close to the poverty line who required help.

The *Blutschutzgesetz* (Law for the protection of German blood and honour) of September 1935 put an end to all this. Aryans were no longer allowed to mix with Jews, and the compulsory transfer of Jews into smaller living quarters made the work that our household staff once did for us, redundant. They were all decent, hard-working people, and with only one exception they continued to visit us under cover of night, to commiserate, to bring some food and to apologise for the cruel deeds of the Nazi government. The exception was Leo the lift driver. He embraced the Nazi Party, wore the brown SA uniform and rode around on the back of open trucks with his party colleagues in the parts of the city where Jews lived, shouting *"Juda verrecke"* – Jews shall perish. However, Leo could not shatter our belief in the many decent Germans, whose friendship and memory I shall always treasure.

There were so many matters that divided me and our German non-Jewish friends – difference in age, in outlook and in the way of making a living. But there was one common bond. A deep affection and respect between one human being to another. The scent of their honest work still lingers on in my memory.

My Heroes

> "Correction does much, but encouragement does more." – Johann Wolfgang von Goethe (1749-1832)

My two grandfathers, Opa Isidor Aufrichtig (1856-1934) and Opa August Schneider (1870-1942), gave direction to my life. Isidor died in December 1934 and so he was spared the years of madness that followed and the full impact of the Holocaust, which destroyed all he had built.

One of my treasured possessions is a piece of black threadbare material. Careful examination of this cloth reveals that in its better days, it was a skull cap. My great-grandfather, grandfather and father wore it for prayer. Opa Isidor would open his bedroom curtain every night, turn east towards Jerusalem and look out of the window into the snow-covered garden to say his evening prayers. I often would discreetly watch him on these occasions. Still today, when reading the *ma'aravoth* (evening blessings), I marvel about their sublime expression of admiration for the beauty of the world and for the privilege to experience Grandfather's loving relationship between Creation and Creator. Opa Isidor went regularly to the *Neue Synagoge,* Europe's second-largest Jewish house of worship, with more than 2000 seats. It was designed by the architect Edwin Oppler, dedicated on 29 September 1872. Grandfather wore a top-hat and pin-striped trousers on the Sabbath and on every major Jewish festival. He had little time for the minor Jewish festivals. He preferred to escape them and instead enjoy a holiday in Venice or the Czech Spa of Karlsbad (Karlovy Vary).

Opa Isidor was a most gifted man, self-taught in Latin and Greek. He had a very large library filled with books by most of the great classical and modern writers, as well as books on philosophy and history, and encyclopedias. He wrote poetry, was good at drawing, and regularly attended opera, concerts and theatre performances. He played skittles and skat (German card game), built up a large business, and had warm relationships with his associates, workers and customers. He paid for the dowry and weddings of his two sisters and in his pre-World War I testament, he left his sisters a "small gift" of 100,000 Goldmark each. He advanced from being the son of a small village innkeeper in Pitschen (Byczyna), Upper Silesia, to a merchant of national importance. His ladies fashion business was in the heart of the city of Breslau in the Junkernstrasse 7. This street was renamed after the World War II to *Ofiar Oświęcimskich* (Victims of Auschwitz). What a strange coincidence!

I used to stand next to Opa Isidor on a leather couch, holding on to his head and shouting into his ear, as he was hard of hearing in his old age. The feel of his short white hair and his embrace are still with me to this day. His difficulty in hearing did not prevent our communication. He would show me the pictures in his most prized books, for instance, the full edition of *Meyers Konversations Lexikon* (a multivolume encyclopedia) and he allowed me to draw in it with coloured pencils despite the protestations of the entire family. When in later years my parents had to downsize and try to sell these books, it was pointed out to me that Grandfather and I had spoiled some of the books and made them unsaleable. It took me years to understand that Opa allowed me to relate to books from an early age and that he taught me that it is not the condition, but the content of books that matters.

There is a beautiful rabbinic story: "When Rabbi Akiba was burned to death, the Romans wrapped him into the parchment of a Torah scroll. As Akiba perished in the flames, the letters and words separated from the parchment of the Torah, so that mankind could grab hold of them and profit from their eternal message."

My grandfather's books were also victims of the Holocaust, but like in the Akiba story, their meaning and message left the paper and have stayed with me to this day. Opa built card houses for me with infinite patience. I enjoyed destroying them, but he rebuilt them again and again, to my great amusement. Indeed, in my life, I learnt from him that we all build card houses and they are often destroyed for us.

The higher we build them, the more easily they fall, but the fun is in the building and in the hours spent together, and so we learn to have patience and peace of mind.

Isidor Aufrichtig died on 29 December 1934 and he was buried on Monday, 31 December in the Jewish cemetery in Breslau-Cosel. The frosty winter's day, the impending 1934 New Year's celebrations, and the harassment of its citizens by the Third Reich, did not prevent hundreds of Opa's Jewish and Christian friends from attending his funeral. Nine months later, in September 1935, Hitler enacted the *Blutschutzgesetz* (Law for the protection of German blood and honour), which would have made such demonstrations of friendship and solidarity impossible.

The modest stone covered with moss, still stands amid the jungle-like Breslau Jewish Cemetery. No-one is left to visit, apart from me and our family. All who knew him have either died, migrated, or were gassed in Hitler's concentration camps. His lasting monument is his life. It still symbolises the once successful and fragile symbiosis of Jewish and German values: "hard work, learning, honesty, integrity, humanity and the search for the meaning of life". He often used to quote the German poet Goethe, who wrote: "To have character means to have the ability to discover good in everything and in every human being." Opa Isidor had this ability. It was an integral part of his being. His memory placed upon me the legacy to carry on the search for the good. A very difficult but most necessary challenge after Auschwitz and after the atrocities in our more recent history.

My mother's father, Opa August Schneider, was a non-practising Protestant. After 1935, the restrictions of the Nuremberg Laws prevented me, a Jewish grandson, and my non-Jewish grandfather to mix. I did not see him very often in my life. We lived in different cities and Jews were not allowed to travel by train without the Gestapo's permission, and that permission was not granted for purely family reasons.

The impact of our early encounters on me was profound. Opa August introduced me to another world. My mother had embraced Judaism in 1928. Her forebears came from German Protestant families who were hereditary farmers in the Lower Lusatia district in Central Germany. Grandfather August's family (Schneider) owned brickworks and peat mines. Grandmother Mienchen's (Wilhelmine) family (Krüger) were graziers. The name Lusatia is derived from the word Luz (Meadow), and most of the farmers in this district lived from harvesting the lush meadows. Grandfather August was not the oldest son in his family, and Grandmother Mienchen, being a woman, had no inheritance rights to her family's farm. Both had a right to income, but not to land. Grandfather had left the land to become a professional soldier in the Prussian Artillery and, on his retirement from the army in 1918, he joined the German Postal Service. In 1815, the Congress of Vienna had separated Lower Lusatia from Saxony and given it to Prussia, so consequently the people of this region were always trying to prove their loyalty to their new Prussian King.

In 1935 Opa August retired and lived in the small city of Guben. He loved horses and often helped the local sawmill to fetch cut fir trees out of the forest. On one occasion, I was able to go with him. We left his home at dawn with four heavy working horses and log-carrying gear, heading for the forest. What a thrill to sit high above the crowd in the streets next to Opa on the carriage, rattling along the streets paved with cobblestones. Opa told me stories about his childhood on the farm, about the Great War, about growing trees, about grazing farm animals and caring for them. We shared breakfast and lunch, which he cut from a large fresh loaf of bread, plastering it with butter and cheese. When we finally arrived in the forest by midday, while the forest-workers loaded the long fir tree logs onto the cart, we fed the horses and then walked together on the soft carpet of moss through the forest.

He made me stop again and again and showed me the beetles under the bark of the trees, and the mushrooms and berries which I would have trampled underfoot had he not pointed them out to me. He made me breathe in the clear aromatic air of the forest, and he opened my eyes to see the colour of the light breaking through the tree-tops and shining on the leaves on the forest floor. He made me fall in love with nature, with the sound of silence and the magnificence and variety of creation. I still remember the feel of the rough skin of his hands and his firm grip on my hand as we walked back together to commence our homeward journey.

I could tighten the brakes as we went downhill, and he encouraged the four strong horses to pull harder when the journey went uphill. We spoke little; the warmth and friendship that had grown between us on this journey did not require many words. The sun was setting, and the steam of perspiration rose from the horses' backs.

We arrived home well after dark, and Oma wanted to put me straight to bed. Opa insisted: "The boy stays with me – he has to learn that animals come first and people second." There was no argument. We fed the horses, dried them and brushed them, gave them fresh straw in the stable and patted their heads, and they in turn pushed against us with their heads, like a gesture of gratitude. I believe we did more than was necessary, and neither of us wanted the day to end. It was a unique quality-time for both of us.

I saw Opa again years later, just a few months before my deportation to the labour camp. He passed through Breslau on his last holiday to the Silesian Mountains (Riesengebirge). At the time, he was suffering from terminal liver cancer. He visited us for a few hours and wanted to take me for a walk. My mother explained that I had to wear the "Yellow Star" on the street and he and I might be hassled by the police or Gestapo. Opa said he would wear the star himself. It was hard to restrain him from expressing his anger in public.

When we parted, he knew we would never meet again and there was still so much left unsaid. On his return home, he would take, wherever he went, the Hitler pictures off the wall. Being challenged by his friends, he replied: "I do not wish to look at this criminal." It was fortunate that the liver cancer brought peace to his troubled soul before the Gestapo could intervene. I still feel drawn to the European forest, its grandeur, solitude and beauty. In its silence, I continue to perceive the wisdom of this great, simple and honest man, who taught me to open my eyes, and to be inspired by the world around me.

Oma Mienchen (1871-1944) was a shy and retiring woman whose life was work. As a young girl, she worked on the family's farm, and her love for the land stayed with her all her life. When I visited the grandparents, Oma was often out, helping in the market gardens, planting or harvesting, collecting mushrooms or berries in the forest. She would bring some of these choice products home, and preserve and store them in the cellar of the house until required. I liked to watch her baking and cooking. She treated each fruit and every product she used with respect and affection, and the results of her cooking endeavours were legendary.

Many people search for a purpose in life. For Oma Mienchen, the purpose of life was just living it to the fullest. The touch of her hand, her quiet manner and affection, were a beacon of light in the troubled world of the 1930s and 1940s. Her goodbye kiss on our last visit to Guben in 1937 remains an abiding blessing throughout my life. She died before her time in 1944 under anaesthetic, during a simple but badly performed operation.

Boycott

> "Where law ends, there tyranny begins." – William Pitt, First Earl of Chatham (1708-78)

Already in 1933, the scene was set for the subsequent twelve years of the Holocaust. The first concentration camp was opened in Dachau near Munich on 22 March. The *Völkischer Beobachter* of 21 March 1933 reads:

> *On Wednesday, the first concentration camp will be opened near Dachau to accommodate 5,000 prisoners. Here, all Communists, and where necessary "Reichsbanner" and Social Democrat functionaries who endanger state security, will be interned together, as their continued stay in normal prisons is proving too great a burden.*

This was followed by a poster, displayed throughout Germany, headed: *"Zur Abwehr! (Be on your guard!)"*. Here are a few short extracts from this poster:

> *The NATIONAL REVOLUTION has smashed the old system to the*

ground. Marxism lies shattered, Germany faces new prosperity. This great German struggle fills INTERNATIONAL JEWRY with hatred and rage. They see their power in Germany coming to an end. They see that they can no longer make Germany into a Soviet Jewish Criminal Colony ... They [Jews in Germany] have appealed to their racial brethren abroad to fight against Germany. They have spread their slander and lies abroad. Therefore, the leaders of the German Liberation Movement have decided to defend themselves against this criminal slander, and from Saturday, April 1st, 1933, at 10am, to observe against all Jewish shops, warehouses, lawyers' practices etc. a boycott. We appeal to you, German men and women, to observe this boycott. Don't buy in Jewish shops and warehouses! Don't engage Jewish lawyers, avoid Jewish doctors! Show the Jews that they cannot disgrace or defile Germany's honour without being punished. Those who ignore this appeal prove that they sympathise with Germany's enemies.

On 1 April 1933 the Nazis implemented "Boycott Day", the boycott of Jewish businesses. Stores owned by Jews were painted with swastikas and the SA prevented customers from entering them. In many instances, the Jewish management and staff were beaten up and harassed.

At the time, the large and loyal mainly non-Jewish staff of my father's business still had the courage to prevent the SA from entering his store. The Jewish owner of the neighbouring store was not so lucky. The SA thugs removed his braces and paraded him along the busy Ohlauerstrasse (Olawska) in Breslau to the amusement of and cheering by the crowd, as he lost his pants and underpants.

Booklet listing the Jewish people to be avoided in Breslau. It was distributed to the public, listing all Jewish businesses and Jewish professionals in Breslau, and warning them "Who buys from a Jew helps World-Bolshevism". Zydowski Instytut Historyczny im. Emanuela Ringelbluma w Warszawie

Zur Abwehr!

nationale Revolution

internationalen Weltjuden

„Sobald ein nichtjüdischer Staat es wagt, uns Juden Widerstand zu leisten, müssen wir in der Lage sein, seine Nachbarn **zum Kriege gegen ihn** zu veranlassen.... Als Mittel dazu werden wir die **öffentliche Meinung** vorschützen. Diese werden wir vorher durch die sogenannte „achte Großmacht", **die Presse** in unserem Sinne bearbeiten. Mit ganz wenig Ausnahmen, die überhaupt nicht in Frage kommen, liegt die ganze Presse der Welt in unseren Händen."

Der Jude lügt, in Deutschland würden Angehörige des jüdischen Volkes grausam zu Tode gefoltert.

Der Jude lügt, es würden diesen Juden die Augen ausgebrannt, die Hände abgehackt, Ohren und Nasen abgeschnitten, ja, selbst die Leichen würden noch zerstückelt.

Der Jude lügt, es würden in Deutschland selbst jüdische Frauen in grauenvoller Weise getötet und jüdische Mädchen vor den Augen ihrer Eltern vergewaltigt.

Der Jude verbreitet diese Lügen in derselben Weise und zu demselben Zwecke, wie er das auch während des Krieges getan hatte. Er will die Welt gegen Deutschland aufwiegeln.

Darüber hinaus fordert er zum

Boykott deutscher Erzeugnisse

auf. Er will damit das Elend der Arbeitslosigkeit in Deutschland noch vergrößern, er will den deutschen Export ruinieren.

Deutsche Volksgenossen! Deutsche Volksgenossinnen!

Die Schuldigen an diesem wahnwitzigen Verbrechen, an dieser niederträchtigen Greuel- und Boykott-Hetze sind die

Juden in Deutschland

Sie haben ihre Rassegenossen im Ausland zum Kampf gegen das deutsche Volk aufgerufen. Sie haben die Lügen und Verleumdungen hinausgemeldet. Darum hat die Reichsleitung der deutschen Freiheitsbewegung beschlossen, in Abwehr der verbrecherischen Hetze

ab Samstag, den 1. April 1933 vormittags 10 Uhr

über alle jüdischen Geschäfte, Warenhäuser, Kanzleien usw.

den **Boykott** zu verhängen.

Dieser Boykottierung Folge zu leisten, dazu rufen wir Euch, deutsche Frauen und Männer, auf!

Kauft nichts in jüdischen Geschäften und Warenhäusern!

Geht nicht zu jüdischen Rechtsanwälten! Meidet jüdische Aerzte!

Wer gegen diese Aufforderung handelt, beweist damit, daß er auf der Seite der Feinde Deutschlands steht.

Paul von Hindenburg!

Adolf Hitler!

Deutsche Vaterland!

Streicher.

This poster was displayed everywhere in Germany on "Boycott Day". Zydowski Instytut

SA (Sturmabteilung, Hitler's private troops) on "Boycott Day". A Short History of the Jewish People, Cecil Roth

The *Reichsverband der Juden* in Deutschland (Central Jewish Representative Body) sent the following telegram to the leaders of the Protestant and Catholic churches:

> *The German Jews, in view of the threats made towards them, hope that soon a word in the name of religion from the Protestant and Catholic churches will be spoken, so that irretrievable damage to man's belief in religion which we share, may be avoided.*

The leader of the Protestant Church, Dr Otto Dibelius (1880-1967), replied on the evening of Boycott Day, after the damage was done, by telegram: "Watching developments with greatest attention; hope that the boycott action will end after this day." A few days later, he showed his true colours in a foreign broadcast, "Protestant Address to America", in which he said: "The overseas reports on these events are a foreign hate message of international Jewry." Dibelius had already written in the Published Church Circular #2 of 3 April 1928: *"I have always considered myself an anti-Semite. It cannot be denied that with all degenerating phenomena of modern civilisation, Judaism plays a leading role."*

The Catholic spokesman, Cardinal Archbishop Dr Adolf Bertram (1859-1945), did not even bother to reply. It is recorded that he said at a bishops' meeting: *"There are immediate issues of much greater importance, schools, the maintaining of Catholic associations, and sterilisation. The Jews are capable of helping themselves."*

On 24 August 1943 Bertram received a letter from a Jewish man who signed himself *Achad Hoq.* This letter gives details about the mass murder of Jews, and it appeals to Bertram, as Chairman of the Conference for Catholic Bishops in Fulda, to act. True to form, Bertram did nothing and the letter was found in the Breslau Palace of the Archbishop after the war. *(Acta Universitatis Wratislaviensis No 1072)*

Following Boycott Day, the Nazi newspaper *V ölkischer Beobachter* refused to take advertisements from Jews. My father appealed to his commanding officer from World War I to intervene. The pleading of this officer for the Nazis to take into consideration my father's service to his German Fatherland in 1914-18 did not fall on deaf ears. However, any success was short-lived. On 13 March 1934, the Germany-wide retail shoe chain Conrad Tack & Cie. AG sent an unsolicited reference to my father and mother greatly praising their managerial skills. It ended with the sentence: "Mr Aufrichtig is relieved from his work because he is non-Aryan, which would make it inappropriate for him to remain in his job." This action was in response to a law passed on 20 January 1934 *(Gesetz zur Ordnung der Nationalen Arbeit)* that prohibited Jews from remaining in leading positions in commerce and industry.

These events greatly impacted on our lives. Money was no longer coming in to support our large household. Few of our non-Jewish friends were willing to risk meeting with us. Jewish family and friends desperately tried to leave Germany, and some managed to do so. By the end of 1935, 60,000 of Germany's 500,000 Jews had fled the country.

The Breslau shoestore of Conrad Tack and Cie Ltd. Universitätsbibliothek Wrocław, Abteilung Gaphische Sammlungen

We had to adjust our lifestyle, so we moved into a four- bedroom apartment in Gabitzstrasse/Adama Prochnika 136, and we even had to sublet two of the four rooms to make ends meet. One of these subtenants, Miss Ottilie Schein, was a teacher of English, French and Spanish. A constant stream of pupils came to her to learn these languages in preparation for immigration.

We sold most of our possessions for very little return, as the market was flooded with goods offered by Jewish families, who were in the same position as us or who were leaving Germany. Our social life became very restricted, as our circle of Jewish friends dwindled and most of our non-Jewish friends kept their distance. More and more restrictions were placed upon us by anti-Jewish legislation. Despite it all, we did not despair. The hostility shown towards us by the outside world was a challenge for our family to close ranks and to respond with great determination to survive the "Thousand-Year Reich".

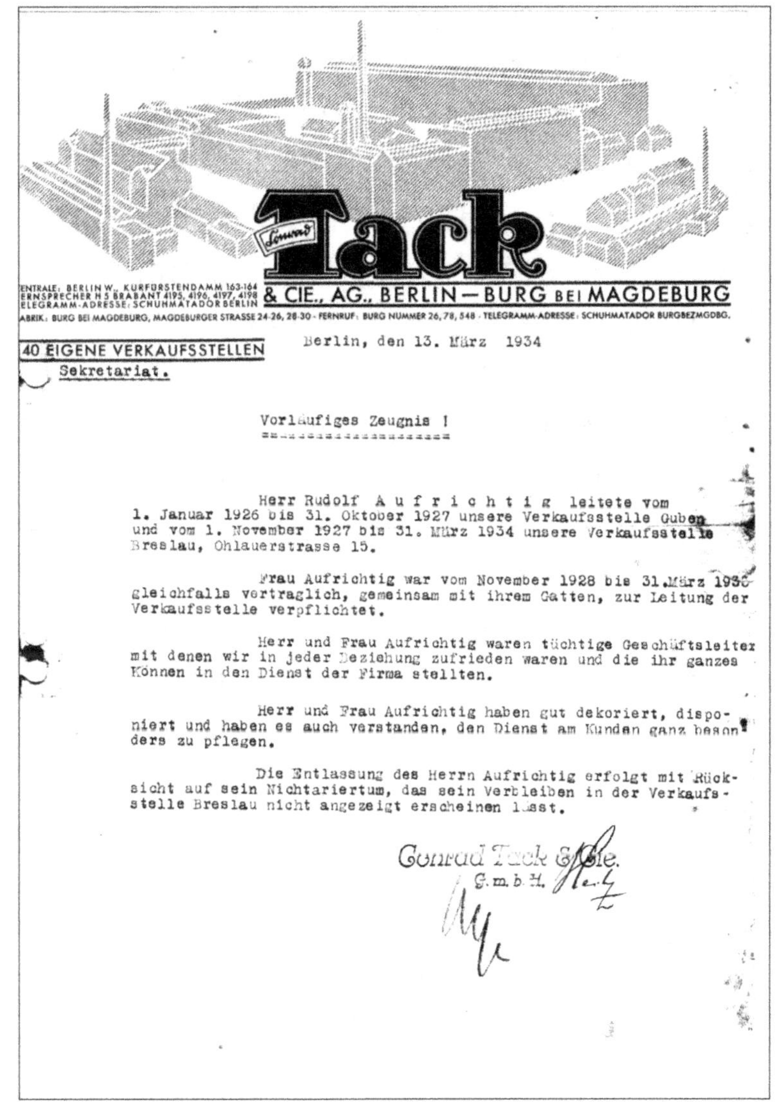

Conrad Tack & CIE., AG., BERLIN — BURG BEI MAGDEBURG

ENTRALE: BERLIN W., KURFÜRSTENDAMM 163-164
ERNSPRECHER H 5 BRABANT 4195, 4196, 4197, 4198
ELEGRAMM-ADRESSE: SCHUHMATADOR BERLIN
ABRIK: BURG BEI MAGDEBURG, MAGDEBURGER STRASSE 24-26, 28-30 · FERNRUF: BURG NUMMER 26, 78, 548 · TELEGRAMM-ADRESSE: SCHUHMATADOR BURGBEZMGDBG.

40 EIGENE VERKAUFSSTELLEN

Sekretariat.

Berlin, den 13. März 1934

Vorläufiges Zeugnis !

Herr Rudolf A u f r i c h t i g leitete vom 1. Januar 1926 bis 31. Oktober 1927 unsere Verkaufsstelle Guben und vom 1. November 1927 bis 31. März 1934 unsere Verkaufsstelle Breslau, Ohlauerstrasse 15.

Frau Aufrichtig war vom November 1928 bis 31.März 1930 gleichfalls vertraglich, gemeinsam mit ihrem Gatten, zur Leitung der Verkaufsstelle verpflichtet.

Herr und Frau Aufrichtig waren tüchtige Geschäftsleiter mit denen wir in jeder Beziehung zufrieden waren und die ihr ganzes Können in den Dienst der Firma stellten.

Herr und Frau Aufrichtig haben gut dekoriert, disponiert und haben es auch verstanden, den Dienst am Kunden ganz besonders zu pflegen.

Die Entlassung des Herrn Aufrichtig erfolgt mit Rücksicht auf sein Nichtariertum, das sein Verbleiben in der Verkaufsstelle Breslau nicht angezeigt erscheinen lässt.

Conrad Tack & Cie.
G.m.b.H.

Letter dated 16 April 1934 from Conrad Tack and Cie. Ltd.

In the evening of 10 May 1933, in many German university cities, Nazi book burning ceremonies were held. In Berlin, this event took place on the

Bebelplatz. The burning of books was planned and hosted by the Nationalist German Student Association. The assembly of the books to be burned had commenced on 6 May. Students dragged books from the library of the Institut für Sexualwissenschaft (Institute for the Science of Sex) into Bebel Square. The German Student Association invited the Propaganda Minister Dr Joseph Goebbels to give an inflammatory speech before the burning ceremony. Members of the Nazi Students' League, the SA, the SS, and Hitler Youth groups also attended this event. Approximately 20,000 books were burned. Books by authors of importance like Karl Marx (1818-83), Heinrich Heine (1797-1856), Heinrich Mann (1871-1950), Erich Maria Remarque (1898-1970), Erich Kästner (1899-1974), Albert Einstein (1879-1955), Siegmund Freud (1856-1939) and many more were among the targeted victims. In 1821 Heinrich Heine wrote these prophetic words in his play *Almansor: "Das war ein Vorspiel nur, dort wo man Bücher verbrennt, verbrennt man auch am Ende Menschen."* (This was merely a prelude, in places where one burns books, human beings will be burnt in the end.)

The burning of books introduced a new educational tool into Nazi Germany called *geistige Gleichschaltung* (parallel thinking). This contrasted with basing intellectual progress on "lateral thinking". The demand by tyrants to make people think in parallel has already been so aptly expressed by Shakespeare in his drama *Julius Caesar:* "He thinks too much; such men are dangerous."

Birthplace in Düsseldorf of Heinrich Heine (1797-1856).

Relatives and friends left many books with us, which they could neither take abroad nor sell. Our library grew and my father would tell me about each book before putting it on the shelves. Initially, I preferred books with pictures, but as I grew older and started to read, books became my best friends. I learnt about the difference between the sexes from medical books and encyclopedias; my interest in our world was aroused by the illustrated science and history books, and the stories of classical literature impacted upon my imagination.

After my father lost his regular occupation, he had to try and make his living by working for various small firms in Breslau, Munich and Berlin, mainly on a temporary basis. The last of these jobs was in a small Jewish-owned shoe store called "Schuhaus Ideal" near the Breslau Hauptbahnhof (Main Railway Station). This job came to an end when the store was vandalised on *Kristallnacht* (Night of Broken Glass) during the night of 9/10 November 1938. My mother had to work as a kitchen hand in one of the Jewish Homes for the Aged.

I had reached the ripe old age of nearly six years, when I commenced schooling in the Private *Vorschule-Gertrud Wohl,*

Lothringerstrasse 8, on 1 April 1935. I had to learn to play on my own after school. My grandmother Emma Aufrichtig (née Schimmelburg) now lived with us. She was slowly dying of stomach cancer. She became my confidante and friend until her death on 19 April 1938.

Non-Jewish friends in high government positions suggested in 1934-35 that we should become baptised, as this might protect us from the full impact of the Nüremberg Laws that were in preparation. There was no way that our family would consider a change of religion for expediency. My mother, who had become Jewish in 1928, pointed out that she was not merely a "Jew by birth", but a Jew by "choice and conviction". Mother had to pay a heavy price. She was regularly invited to the Gestapo office for counselling, that she should divorce my father and shed the burden of her Jewish family. She steadfastly refused. The Gestapo told her to think about her Jewishness until her next monthly meeting with them. They also pointed out to Mother that "she was even worse than a born Jew".

Jewish family and friends counselled us that we should emigrate as soon as possible, but my parents were not prepared to abandon my dying grandmother. Furthermore, Paul von Hindenburg was still President of Germany, until his death on 2 August 1934. He was the great German hero of World War I under whose command my father fought in the German Army in 1914-18, and who promised:" *Der Dank des Vaterlandes ist Euch gewiss"* (You can be assured of the gratitude of the Fatherland). There seemed to be no reason to panic and abandon ship.

These discussions took place out of my and my grandmother's earshot, which was a totally unnecessary precaution. At that stage of my life, I still had full confidence that my parents would always be able to protect me from all of life's vicissitudes.

Gathering of the Storm

"Alea iacta est." (The die is cast) - Julius Caesar (100-49 BCE)

A significant change in anti-Jewish legislation occurred during the years 1935-37. Basic human rights were taken away from Jews during these years, while in previous years, legislation mainly targeted economic matters. The most significant of these latter laws were the Nuremberg Laws which included *Blutschutzgesetz.* Jews lost citizen rights, were no longer permitted to have inter-marital and extra-marital relationships with non-Jews, could no longer serve in the German Army and were forbidden to hoist a German flag. Some 1425 Jews received prison sentences for *Rassenschande* (the defilement of German blood).

Usually, the prisoners were transferred from prison to concentration camps, which was the end of the road. Dachau concentration camp could no longer cope with the ever-increasing number of prisoners and so more concentration camps were established: Sachsenhausen and Oranienburg in July 1936, and Buchenwald on the Ettersberg near Weimar in July 1937. Now it became crystal clear that there was no point for Jews to stay in Germany any longer. (After World War II, the Soviet Occupation Authority continued to use the Buchenwald concentration camp, 1945 to 1950. They renamed it: NKVD Special Camp number 2.)

In 1933 approximately 37,000 Jews left Germany (74 per cent went to European countries; 19 per cent to Palestine; 7 per cent to overseas countries). In 1934 approximately 23,000 Jews left Germany (35 per cent went to European countries; 37 per cent to Palestine; 28 per cent to overseas countries). In 1935 approximately 21,000 Jews left Germany (31 per cent went to European countries; 36 per cent to Palestine; 33 per cent to overseas countries). In 1936 approximately 25,000 Jews left Germany (20 per cent went to European countries; 34 per cent to Palestine; 46 per cent to overseas countries). In 1937 approximately

23,000 Jews left Germany (27 per cent went to European countries; 11 per cent to Palestine; 60 per cent to overseas countries). In 1938-39 approximately 15,000 Jews of Polish nationality living in Germany were shunted by the Nazi government illegally into Poland, an action that led to *Kristallnacht* (9 November 1938) and in these two years until the beginning of World War II, approximately 140,000 German Jews fled or emigrated from Germany. A census on 17 May 1939 confirmed that there were still 213,930 Jews living in Germany. About 20,000 survived the war; the rest were murdered in the various concentration camps. This should not have been unexpected, as Hitler publicly promised in his speech in the Reichstag on 30 January 1939: "If the international finance-Jewry inside and outside Europe should succeed in plunging the nations into a world war yet again, then the outcome will not be the victory of Jewry, but rather the annihilation of the Jewish race in Europe!"

The contribution of Britain towards the Jewish dilemma was about as helpful as Hitler's speech in the German Parliament. On 20 July 1939, in the House of Commons, Lt. Col. Sir Arnold Wilson, presenting the Arab case, made no attempt to deny "the material benefit which has accrued to the inhabitants of Palestine" because of Jewish immigration. But he added: "I lived long enough among Persians and Arabs to know that they are not exclusively concerned with material benefits ... Nationalism is a growing force, with its good as well as bad sides. There is no possibility whatever of the Arabs accepting, as consolation for the loss of their homeland, a few more cinemas and a few more dentists, and two pairs of shoes where before they had one pair or none. There is no solution by that road here or elsewhere." The consequence of this debate in the British Parliament was that Britain produced a White Paper on British Rule in Palestine. It held that Jews were prohibited from buying more land outside their existing settlements and that Jewish migration to Palestine was to be restricted to 75,000 in the coming four-year period to 1944. The British believed that this would keep the Jews as a permanent minority in Palestine, and British authorities were determined to turn back ships carrying "illegal" Jewish immigrants to Palestine – a problem that would intensify during the war in Europe.

Several countries refused to give shelter to Jews who fled Nazi Germany. These Jews had no option but to return to Germany. On 23 January 1938, the Gestapo issued an order to place these returning Jews into concentration camps. About 1500 Jews ended up in the camps during 1938, because their chosen country refused to accept them on arrival; most of them perished.

In preparation for emigration, German Jews learnt English, Spanish, cake making, jewellery fabrication, millinery, Rabbinic practice, even how to play bridge. From time to time, a few fortunate members of our family and Jewish friends came to say goodbye before leaving for abroad.

There was Aunt Hennie Bernstein, who had been educated in a Swiss finishing school and therefore found employment as a governess for children with a wealthy Jewish family in Athens.

Cousin Ilse Redlich left with a *Kindertransport* to England, where she had to work as a housemaid, and from there she moved on to Australia. Ilse's brother Walter and her parents stayed behind, and were exterminated in 1943.

Walter Monasch, the son of my father's cousin Hans Monasch, came on a short visit to Breslau to say goodbye on behalf of his branch of the family. Hans Monasch's first cousin, the Australian General Sir John Monash, had died on 8 October 1931. There was little contact with the General and the remaining members of his German family and so Hans Monasch and his family ended up in Chicago, USA, making a living by selling encyclopedias and silver cutlery door to door.

My father's cousin Hilde Aufrichtig, who was a lawyer in Breslau, emigrated to England, where her German law qualifications were not recognised. Her mother, Hedwig Aufrichtig, who accompanied her, cooked and baked for Manchester society, so that Hilde could obtain an English law degree. After her mother died, Hilde studied classical Chinese literature and taught this subject at university.

Several family members and friends had emigrated to South America. The older generation kept in touch with us, but the next generation no longer spoke or wrote in German and consequently family contact ceased.

My parents had delayed emigration as they did not want to abandon my grandparents in Germany, who were "too old" to be accepted by any overseas country. Emigration finally became the main topic of conversation in our family, after Grandmother Emma had succumbed to stomach cancer on 19 April 1938. Shanghai, Australia, USA, the Dominican Republic, South Africa and South American countries were all under consideration. It was too late. Hitler's worldwide warmongering and the increase in the tempo of German-Jewish persecution was an incentive to try and leave Germany at all costs. However, Jews without money and without the appropriate language skills were not a favoured import commodity, and so our plans to leave Germany came to nought.

Legislation during the second half of 1938 put further stumbling blocks into our way, such as:

1) (26 April 1938) All cash and property owned by Jews worth more than 5000 marks had to be declared to the Gestapo and bank accounts were blocked.
2) (17 May 1938) Special questions on racial origin were included in the census, thereby cataloguing all potential victims for future extermination.
3) (23 July 1938) Legislation was passed forcing Jews to always carry a special Jewish Identity Card.
4) (12 November 1938) Jewish citizens of Germany had to pay collectively a penalty *(Sühneabgabe)* of one billion marks for the assassination of Ernst Eduard von Rath on 7 November 1938.
5) (16 November 1938) Passports had to be surrendered. The issue of new passports became

restricted and they were marked with the letter "J" for Jew.

6) (1 January 1939) Jewish men had to add the given name "Israel" and women "Sarah" to their name.

7) (21 February 1939) Jews had to hand over to the government all gold, silver and precious stones in their possession.

Some German Jewish families sent their children abroad. I was nine years old in 1938 and there was debate in our home whether I should leave Germany with a *Kindertransport* to Holland. After long deliberations, my parents reached the conclusion that it would be safer for me to stay with them. Their reasoning was wrong, but the result of this flawed decision saved my life. Most of the children who were sent from Germany to Holland were the first to be deported to extermination camps when Hitler invaded Holland.

Our luxurious home in Breslau, Charlottenstrasse 8, in which the family had lived since 1916, had to be vacated on 20 July 1937 because my parents could no longer afford to live there. The staff required to maintain the place were not allowed to work for us after the enactment of the *Blutschutzgesetz* in 1935. I thought these people were my friends and I had problems understanding the changes. We once believed that we were German citizens of the Jewish faith. It took all of us some time to learn that now we were only Jews.

The history professor Heinrich von Treitschke proclaimed in 1879: *"Die Juden sind unser Unglück"* (The Jews are our misfortune).Hitler used this academic pronouncement to claim that anti-Semitism had preceded his government by 54 years and that now it was high time to take some positive action in this matter.

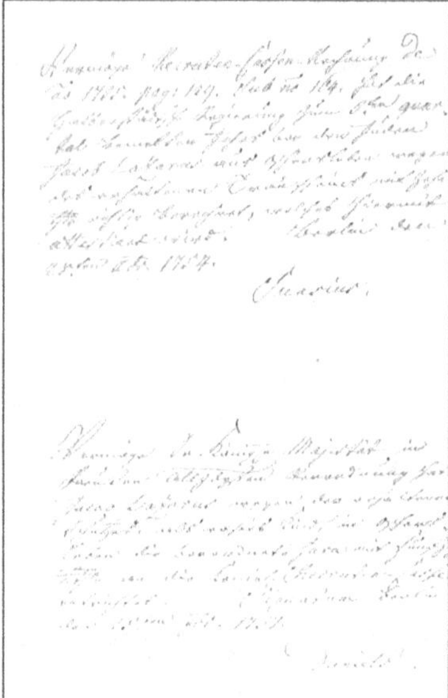

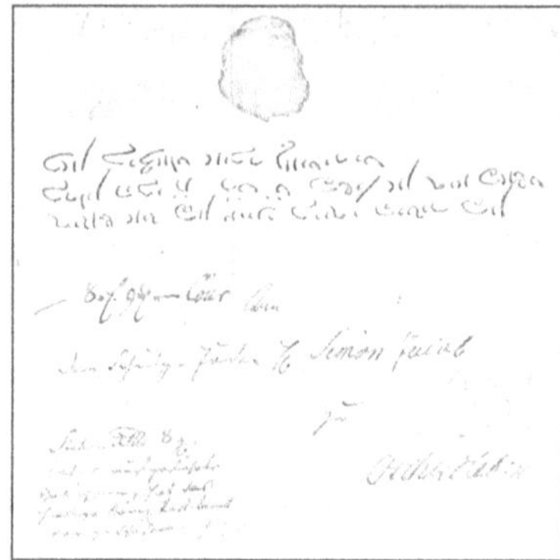

Transfer of house owned by 'Protected Jew' Simon Jacob (my great-great-great-grandfather) on 20 October 1754.

Gesetz-Sammlung
für die
Königlichen Preußischen Staaten.

No. 5.

(No. 80.) Edikt, betreffend die bürgerlichen Verhältnisse der Juden in dem Preußischen Staate. Vom 11ten März 1812.

Wir Friedrich Wilhelm, von Gottes Gnaden König von Preußen 2c. 2c.

haben beschlossen, den jüdischen Glaubensgenossen in Unserer Monarchie eine neue, der allgemeinen Wohlfahrt angemessene Verfassung zu ertheilen, erklären alle bisherige, durch das gegenwärtige Edikt nicht bestätigte Gesetze und Vorschriften für die Juden für aufgehoben und verordnen wie folget:

§. 1. Die in Unsern Staaten jetzt wohnhaften, mit General-Privilegien, Naturalisations-Patenten, Schutzbriefen und Konzessionen versehenen Juden und deren Familien sind für Einländer und Preußische Staatsbürger zu achten.

§. 2. Die Fortdauer dieser ihnen beigelegten Eigenschaft als Einländer und Staatsbürger wird aber nur unter der Verpflichtung gestattet:

daß sie fest bestimmte Familien-Namen führen,

und

daß sie nicht nur bei Führung ihrer Handelsbücher, sondern auch bei Abfassung ihrer Verträge und rechtlichen Willens-Erklärungen der deutschen oder einer andern lebenden Sprache, und bei ihren Namens-Unterschriften keiner andern, als deutscher oder lateinischer Schriftzüge sich bedienen sollen.

§. 3. Binnen sechs Monaten, von dem Tage der Publikation dieses Edikts an gerechnet, muß ein jeder geschützte oder konzessionirte Jude vor der

Jahrgang 1812. E Obrigkeit

(ausgegeben zu Berlin den 17ten März 1812.)

The edict by Friedrich Wilhelm King of Prussia.
Bildarchiv Preussischer Kulturbesitz

My great-great-grandfather Leiser Schimmelburg (1791-1838) was the first member of our family who ceased to be merely a *Schutzjude* (Protected Jew) when he became a Prussian citizen in accordance with the Emancipation edict of 11 March 1812 issued by Friedrich Wilhelm III (1770-1840), King of Prussia.

Leiser and his brother Julius fought in the Prussian Cavalry against Napoleon

I in the Leipzig Battle of the Nations (16-19 October 1813). Leiser received a written commendation for bravery from the Prussian General Ludwig Adolf Wilhelm von Lützow; Julius was killed in action. The defeat of Napoleon at this battle forced Napoleon to abdicate on 6 April 1814 and to go into exile on the island of Elba. Napoleon stayed on Elba for only 100 days and he returned to govern France once again. He was finally defeated in the battle of Waterloo on 18 June 1815. He was then exiled to the island of St Helena, where he died on 5 May 1821.

After this war, Leiser donated beautiful new stained-glass windows for the city church of his hometown Oschersleben in memory of his brother Julius and in memory of all the other fallen soldiers in the Napoleonic wars. In response, the citizens of Oschersleben affixed a black marble plaque on the outside of the church wall expressing the gratitude of the citizens of this city to the "Jew Leiser Schimmelburg". This plaque was removed in the early 1930s on the orders of the Hitler government.

My great-grandfather Jacob Schimmelburg (1823-1907) served in the Prussian Cavalry in the 1870-71 Franco-Prussian war. A beautiful French cavalry pistol which he had brought back as booty from this war graced a wall of our lounge room for many years. This muzzle-loading cavalry pistol was also a victim of the Holocaust. When Jews were no longer allowed to own firearms, my father stuck it into our kitchen stove, burning off all the wooden parts, and the remaining metal parts Father and I dropped into the street drains after dark, making sure that no one was watching us in the process.

Marktkirche St. Nikolai Oschersleben. Günther Blume. Oschersleben war uns Heimat, L. Bittner

Great-grandfather Jacob Schimmelburg on his 75th birthday, 24 September 1898.

My father served for four years with great enthusiasm in the German Army in World War I. He was wounded three times and yet he continued with frontline service. The almost complete collection of the German war newspaper *Deutsche Kriegszeitung,* with its many photographs of military action, kept me interested in this sombre part of European history. I also used to admire Father's Iron Cross, as well as his Honour Cross of World War I and I enjoyed playing with his steel helmet until the Hitler years.

The *Ehrenkreutz des Weltkrieges 1914-1918* (Honour Cross of the World War) was created by the Third Reich on 13 July 1934. Hitler was not yet Führer – he was merely Chancellor, and Field-Marshal Paul von Hindenburg was the President of Germany. It was the last occasion that the Third Reich had no option but to acknowledge that approximately 110,000 Jewish men served in the German Army in World War I and 12,000 of them were killed in action.

I remember my grandmother Emma from her death bed watching me lovingly play with model soldiers. My ninth birthday preceded her death by three days. I had asked her to give me the model of *Reichsmarschall* Hermann Goering as a birthday present. My parents were outraged that I could ask for this and they were even more bewildered that my grandmother was prepared to give it to me. Was it so surprising, if you consider the close connection of our family history with the history of Germany? Grandmother Emma wanted to show her love for me to the very last, and whatever I would have asked from her, I would have received as her last birthday present without question.

The family house at Magdeburgerstrasse 16, Oschersleben in 1850 and 2003. Woman on left was my great-great-grandmother Therese Schimmelburg.

My father Rudolf Aufrichtig with his parents Emma and Isidor Aufrichtig in 1915.

Maybe she considered that the fat, drug-addicted Goering was nothing but a toy, when compared with three generations of our family's battle-hardened Jewish Prussian soldiers.

Grandmother may have felt a little more at ease, had she known at the time that Hermann Goering had a younger brother Albert Günther Goering (1895-1966) who was a German businessman. Hermann and Albert's parents were Heinrich Ernst Goering (1839-1913) and Franziska Tiefenbrunn (1859-1923) who came from Bavarian peasant stock. The Goering family lived with their children's aristocratic godfather of Jewish decent, Ritter Hermann von Epenstein. Von Epenstein began an affair with Franziska Goering about a year before Albert's birth. The strong physical resemblance between von Epenstein and Albert Goering led many people to believe that these two were father and son. If this is true, it would indicate that Albert Goering had Jewish paternal ancestry. Albert Goering is believed to have saved hundreds of Jews and political dissidents during World War II. Goering's humanitarian efforts are recorded in a book by William Hastings Burke called *Thirty-Four.* A review of the book in *The*

Jewish Chronicle concluded with a call for Albert Goering to be honoured at the Yad Vashem memorial.

Rudolf Aufrichtig in Saint Mihiel at the French Front in February 1918.

A service for German-Jewish soldiers in Lubias, WWI 1916.

Service for German Jewish soldiers killed in WWI, February 1938, Synagogue Oranienburgerstrasse, Berlin. Bildarchiv Abraham Pisarek

Oma Emma knew in her heart that she was dying and that she would not be alive to celebrate my bar mitzvah with me in four years. So, she left for me a savings bank book containing all her money, to be given to me as her present on my bar mitzvah. She had attached to this book a most touching and loving letter: "Learn everything life has to offer you in its fullness and completeness." She could not have anticipated what life had to offer me, and that her request to explore its fullness and completeness would enabled me to find a little of the good, despite everything, even if I had to search for it long and hard at times. Fortunately, she could not foresee that at the time of my bar mitzvah the savings account would be blocked and made worthless by the Nazi government, that synagogues would be destroyed and Jewish public worship prohibited, and that the Wannsee Conference would plan the systematic murder of all European Jews. There was not to be a bar mitzvah for me!

The Inferno

> *"Recht ist, was dem deutschen Volke nützt, Unrecht, was ihm schadet."* (Law is, what is useful to the German people, injustice is what is harmful for it.) – Hans Michael Frank (1900-46)

Until 9 November 1938, persecution of the Jews in Germany may not have been ethical, but it followed the letter of the law. Hans Michael Frank was a German lawyer. He already worked for the Nazi party during the 1920s and 1930s. He later became Hitler's personal lawyer. In 1933, Frank became Nazi Germany's chief jurist and Governor-General of occupied Poland. Between 1939 and 1945 Frank instituted a reign of terror against the Polish and Jewish population of Poland through systematic plunder, brutal economic exploitation and finally mass murder.

In my childlike imagination, I assumed that the Neue Synagoge in Breslau had always been there. I still find it hard to accept that this impressive building was only tolerated for 46 years by the citizens of Breslau. Until the beginning of the nineteenth century, synagogues in most European cities were not allowed to be built on a street frontage and their building height was limited to two storeys. With the emancipation of the Jews, these restrictions were relaxed in the mid-1800s. This resulted in a building boom of very large Jewish houses of worship.

The Neue Synagoge in Breslau was designed by the architect Edwin Oppler (1831-1880) and dedicated on 29 September 1892. It was, with more than 2000 seats, one of the largest in Europe. It had a grand modern pipe organ, an excellent professional choir, and the first tenor of the Breslau Opera House, Selmar Steifmann (stage name: Cerini, 1861-1923), was the cantor of this synagogue for many years. The resident rabbis were great orators and scholars, and the occasional sermons given by academic rabbis from the Breslau Rabbinic Seminary always provided added interest. The synagogue's 60-metre-high dome and the towers at the four corners of the building were visible all over the city. On the Jewish High Holydays it was filled beyond capacity, making it necessary for the community to conduct overflow services in the city's Grossen Konzerthaussaal and Youth Services in the Kammermusiksaal of the Breslauer Philharmonie in Gartenstrasse/Karola Świerczewskiego.

It was always an unforgettable event for me to join my parents and grandparents for services in this sanctuary. Grandfather attended these services dressed in grey pin-striped trousers, morning-coat and top hat, and he had a first-class seat in the front part of the building, which enabled me to see and hear everything from close-up. In the afternoon of the Day of Atonement, I was given just enough pocket money to enable me to buy two small bunches of violets from the flower vendors who had gathered on the street outside the synagogue and to bring them as a present to Mother and Grandmother seated in the ladies gallery. I was not alone in this act. The scent of well over a thousand bunches of violets that filled the synagogue for the rest of the long day's service still lingers on in my memory.

This Great Synagogue was filled on most occasions, especially during the Hitler years after 1933. It became much more than a place of worship; it became a place of refuge. One exchanged information on ways and means for survival, and one looked anxiously around to learn which familiar faces had disappeared, who had been lucky enough to emigrate. My sights were fixed on yet another target. At every Friday night service, the best male and female students in Hebrew and Jewish studies were called up during the service to flank the cantor during the Kiddush prayer. They were given their own small cup of wine to drink at the appropriate time. It was a unique opportunity to stand in front of over 2000 worshippers as a proud Jew, at a time when Judaism and Jews were defamed. In hindsight, it is hard in our present more secular society to believe that so many worshippers could have gathered at normal Sabbath services.

Neue Synagoge (New Synagogue) in Breslau exterior. Herder Institut e.V. Marburg, Bildarchiv

My moment of glory arrived on Friday, 4 November 1938. At this service, the synagogue building was packed to capacity. It was a farewell service for the senior rabbi, Dr Hermann Vogelstein (1870-1942), who emigrated to the UK and later to the USA. The service on Saturday, 5 November 1938 was a welcome service for the new rabbi, Dr Reinhold Lewin, who came to Breslau with his family from the Jewish community of Königsberg/Kalinengrad in East Prussia. Rabbi Lewin's son Ulli became a good friend of mine until the entire family was deported and exterminated in Auschwitz. None of us could have anticipated that this exciting Shabbat was to be the last in this great synagogue.

Neue Synagoge (New Synagogue) in Breslau interior. Herder Institut e.V. Marburg, Bildarchiv

The following week on Wednesday, 9 November, a non-Jewish army friend of my father's from World War I called on us. He had since joined the Nazi Party, but he continued to respect my father for his leadership and his bravery which had earned Father the "Iron Cross". He implored my father to go with my mother and me before sunrise on Thursday into a nearby forest and not to return home until sunset. He would not explain the reason for his strange advice, nor would he stay, but he asked for my father's trust and begged him to follow his advice. My father returned his kindness by lecturing him that as he did not run away from the enemy during his four years of service in the Great War, he was not going to start now to run away from his own home.

During the night of 9 to 10 November an inferno destroyed the Neue Synagoge and it signalled the beginning of the end for German Jews. On Thursday morning, 10 November, the wife of our Jewish neighbour called on us, crying bitterly. She told my mother that her husband and most Jewish men in the neighbourhood had been dragged from their homes, loaded onto trucks and driven away. No one knew where to. She suggested that I should find my father who had already left for work, as the Nazis were picking up Jewish men off the streets. The synagogues were burning and all Jewish shops were ransacked.

I was on the way to school along Hohenzollernstrasse/ Zaporoska and I walked past a Jewish-owned confectionary store. A friendly German policeman who was guarding the vandalised store picked up a handful of chocolates from the street and gave them to me to eat and enjoy. He warned me to make sure that there were no glass splinters in the chocolates.

I was one of the few children arriving at the school. The female teacher sent me straight back home. It was an emotional scene at the school, as the Gestapo had already picked up some of her male colleagues for deportation. Arriving home, my mother sent me into town to look for my father in his business, but I could not find him. The Jewish shoe store where he worked was destroyed, and Father, as we found out later, had gone straight to the insurance company to claim for damages. On the way home, I passed the Neue Synagoge. I had never seen such an inferno. The shouting mob around the building was frightening and intimidating, and made me want to return home as quickly as possible. Along the way, I passed many ransacked Jewish businesses. One that stood out was the large wine shop in the Höfchenstrasse/ Tadeusza Zielinkiego. The Nazis must have smashed every bottle of wine in the shop, and the pavement in front of the shop was awash with a mixture of white and red wines, champagne and liquors. An unforgettable smell!

Finally, my parents and I took the advice given by the non-Jewish friend the previous night, and we went into hiding in the nearby forest. Little was spoken as we walked endlessly along the quiet paths. It was cold and wet November weather. We encountered only a few people along the way. Indeed, we did not wish to meet anyone, as the possibility of Nazi mop-up operations was on our minds. Mid-afternoon we dared to climb a lookout, and from a hilltop we could see the whole city of Breslau and the synagogue burning. As we walked on, the sound of an explosion made us turn around again. Just smoke! Where was the great dome of the building? Maybe we had not looked properly! The next day gave us the answer.

The following passage is an excerpt from an article about this event in the Breslau daily paper, *Schlesische Zeitung:* "Thousands of fellow Germans who roamed the streets of Breslau, said goodbye without any regret from the rubble and ashes of the synagogue, which are the last reminders of a time when Breslau was for long enough the domicile of Judaism. For long enough, National Socialism has not used the rifle and watched the outrageous behaviour of these impudent invaders. Now, at the deathbed of a new blood sacrifice, National Socialism has acted, and from this action, the Jews in Breslau and the Jews anywhere in the German Reich will never recover."

Neue Synagoge Breslau burning on Kristallnacht (9 November 1938). Erwin Hirschberg

The Breslau Gestapo office reported to the Berlin headquarters: "Three synagogues and three social facilities burnt to the ground. Five hundred shops and department stores, as well as ten Jewish restaurants were demolished; thirty-five other Jewish businesses destroyed, and approximately six hundred Jewish men were arrested and sent to concentration camp."

We kept on walking until it was dark, and then returned home. The neighbours told us that no one had called for my father. His army friend must have succeeded in saving him from deportation. Others were not so lucky.

My father's cousin Richard Bernstein returned from his sojourn in the concentration camp Buchenwald and died a few days later in the Breslau Jewish hospital from the consequences of his stay in this camp. The Gestapo had destroyed Richard's department store in the nearby little town of Oels/Olesnica on 9 November. The merchandise was lying around in the street. In his absence, the local police served an order on his 70-year-old mother to clean up the store. Tante Meta Bernstein, as always, called on us for help, and so my mother went to Oels to try and clean up the mess single-handed. Some of the locals were giving her verbal abuse and were throwing glass at her. Mother had to call for the help of the local police who stood guard while mother was cleaning up. The family did not know much about Richard's business, and so my parents called a cousin, Kurt Schimmelburg, a lawyer, to try and sort out the legal problems. Kurt stayed with us for a day. What a joke! He found out that Richard had sold his business to a German Aryan on the 8th of November and the Gestapo had hit at the wrong target. It was a good lesson for the new owner of Richard's business to learn about the state of justice in the Third Reich.

Kristallnacht was well planned. The synagogues were set alight during the night between Wednesday and Thursday. Sabbath commenced on Friday evening and the ruins of the burned synagogues were still smouldering. Ninety-one Jews had been killed; 30,000 Jewish men were arrested and sent to the concentration camps of Dachau, Buchenwald and Sachsenhausen; 1,000 synagogues had been destroyed; 7,000 businesses owned by Jews had been destroyed and had to be closed.

What to do? Should Sabbath services be cancelled? Jews were no longer allowed to hire halls for religious services owned by non-Jews. Breslau had a Jewish Association founded on 11 January 1871 called *Die Gesellschaft der Freunde* (The Association of Friends). This association's program was to engender friendship between people and to "plant into the minds of members and friends the idea of creating eternal peace between nations". The Gesellschaft der Freunde club building had the largest banquet hall in the inner city of Breslau. It was in this hall that the Sabbath eve service was held on Friday, 11 November 1938. Was the service to be held in the Jewish Orthodox or in the Jewish Progressive format? The leader of German Jewry, Rabbi Dr Leo Baeck, aptly said at the time: "Orthodox and progressive are merely adjectives, the noun is always Judaism." The hall was packed and the service was highly emotional. Congregants took stock whose families were still intact and whose were broken. Men and women sat together wherever there was room. Women cried, not knowing at the time what had happened to their husbands. History seemed to have repeated itself. The Orthodox Rabbi Gedalia Tiktin (1808-86) and the Progressive Rabbi Manuel Joel (1826-90) had together dedicated the Neue Synagoge in 1892, and the Progressive Rabbi Dr Reinhold Lewin and the Orthodox Rabbi B. Hamburger jointly conducted a farewell service for all the destroyed or vandalised Breslau synagogues in 1938.

The words Orthodox (Greek: orthos=correct; doxa=opinion) as applied to Judaism, and Catholic (Greek: universal) applied to Christianity are offensive and no longer have a place in twenty-first century religion. Jews who still claim to have the *correct* Jewish belief to the exclusion of all others, and Christians who still claim that their religious teaching should be applied *universally,* have failed to understand the lessons of the Holocaust.

Ulli, the son of the newly appointed Rabbi Dr Reinhold Lewin, was my school friend. We played together in the rabbi's apartment that overlooked the smouldering ruin of the Neue Synagoge, and we often peered through the curtain, gazing into the rubble of this great building. I remember Ulli's father moving us gently away from the window, saying: "We shall survive and then we shall have to build again." Reinhold Lewin and his family, as well as his orthodox colleague B. Hamburger were both killed in a concentration camp in 1943.

(I was one of the founders of Temple David in Perth in 1952 and was its cantor, choir master, president, board member and honorary life member. I have helped to 'build again' by remembering the destruction of the Breslau synagogue, and the family of Rabbi Reinhold Lewin.)

Every coin has two sides, and there are two sides to every event. The historical importance of *Kristallnacht* should not be overlooked. The events leading up to and following *Kristallnacht* are not so well known, but they need to be considered to understand this most significant part of German-Jewish history.

On 4 November 1938 Dr Hans Joseph Maria Globke (1898-1973), co-author of the Nuremberg Laws, called a conference in his office to plan ridding Germany of its Jews, indeed of all non-German-Aryan elements of the population. A decision was taken to commence with this task as soon as appropriate, but no detailed plan was made.

THE MACCABEAN NOVEMBER, 1963

● Pictured at the Temple Dedication are (L. to R.): Mr. E. Silbert (Vice-President), Mr. K. Arkwright (Cantor), Rabbi G. Rubens, Dr. R. Taft (President), Mr. K. Gottschalk (Life Member) and Mr. H. Boas (Life Member).

Temple David in Perth, Western Australia that I helped found in 1952. Maccabean Newspaper, Perth, WA

The interior of Temple David now.

The Polish Intelligence Service reported to its government about this German plan. The Polish government was concerned that 17,000 Jews living in Germany, and 30,000 in Austria with Polish passports, would be returned to Poland. This was not acceptable to Poland. The Polish government therefore decided on 6 October 1938 to declare that all Polish passports of its citizens living permanently abroad would become invalid from 29 October 1938. The German government reacted promptly. Hermann Goering, in his capacity as Prime Minister of Prussia, invited ministers to his office on the 14 October 1938, stating: "The Jewish question has to be tackled with all means and the Jews have to be excluded from the economy." However, the meeting ended without a detailed plan of action.

On 24 October 1938, Joachim von Ribbentrop, Germany's Foreign Minister, took the initiative and summoned Jozef Lipski, Poland's Ambassador in Berlin, to his office, requesting that Poland take back within 48 hours, all Jews living in Germany with a Polish passport. Other demands were also made, such as the return of the city of Gdansk to Germany, etc. The Polish Ambassador did not reply in time. To beat the expiry date of the passports (29 October 1938), Reinhardt Heydrich, the German Chief of Security, arranged for Gestapo and police to collect the 18,000 Polish Jews living in Germany and to drive them illegally across the Polish border. The Polish border guards were unprepared, and consequently Heydrich's "*Polenaktion*" was successful. After Poland had closed the border, only 1800 Jews had to be brought back into Germany.

Among the evicted Jews was the tailor Sendel Grynszpan, and his wife and daughter from Hannover. Sendel's son Herschel, who was born in Hannover in 1921, was at the time staying with an uncle in Paris. On 7 November 1938 at 9.35am, Herschel called on the German Embassy in Paris, and asked to hand important documents to a *Legationsrat* (Councillor of the Embassy). He was ushered into the room of *Legationsrat,* Ernst vom Rath. Herschel shot vom Rath, was apprehended by the French police, interrogated and imprisoned.

The interrogation was conducted by a policeman, François Collet Autret, a French judge, Jean Tesnière, and most irregularly by the Chancellor of the Paris German Embassy. The protocol stated that Grynszpan said that he shot vom Rath to avenge his Jewish co-religionists. Ernst vom Rath died on 9 November 1938. At that time, Hitler was giving a dinner in the Munich Town Hall for his *Alte K ämpfer* (Old Guard) to commemorate the 25th anniversary of his failed attempt to gain power in 1923. The signal to organise *Kristallnacht* Germany-wide within a matter of hours was a most hateful speech of Goebbels at this celebration. The pogrom was carried out by the SA, SS, Gestapo, Criminal and General Police; the Minister of Justice gave instructions to the courts to abstain from any legal investigations or actions in this matter. On the eve of 10 November, a report to the government read: "In Germany, Austria, the Sudetenland and a day later in Danzig, 91 Jews were killed, 30,000 Jewish men were placed into concentration camps, 7,500 Jewish businesses demolished, and 267 synagogues were either burned or demolished."

The pogrom was under the patronage of Goebbels, because it was for him a welcome opportunity to re-legitimise himself. Hitler had asked him in summer 1938 to either resign or to give up his Czech mistress, the actress Lida Baarova (also known as Ludmila Babkova) (1914-2000). Hitler was the godfather of Goebbels' children and for Goebbels to flaunt a mistress, and a Czech one at that, was unacceptable.

Goebbels provoked, with *Kristallnacht,* the criticism of his peers. The minutes of a meeting on 12 November 1938 record that Goering said: "I would have preferred that you would have beaten 200 Jews to death and not destroyed such values." Economy Minister Walther Funk rang Goebbels, saying: "Are you crazy to make such a mess of things? One must be ashamed to be a German. We are losing our prestige abroad. I am trying to conserve national wealth, and you throw it out of the window. If this thing does not stop immediately, I'll throw the whole mess back at you." Himmler made a memorandum note: "The order was given by the Propaganda Directorate, and I suspect that Goebbels, in his craving for power, which I noticed long ago, and in his empty-headedness, started this pogrom at a time when the foreign political situation is very grave ... When I asked the Führer about it, I had the impression that he did not know anything about these events."

The next to complain was Goering. He motivated Hitler to hold two meetings on 10 November 1938, and to exclude Goebbels from all future active persecution of the Jews. Goebbels also lost the right to comment on foreign affairs without clearance from Ribbentrop. Goebbels' suggestion to repair the economic damage was to make the German Jews pay one billion marks restitution, and to conduct a show-trial of Herschel Grynszpan. This was accepted by Hitler.

However, France did not allow Grynszpan to be extradited to Germany.

The French Minister of Justice most inappropriately advised the Paris German Embassy: "At any time questions on the progress on the preparation of the trial will be answered confidentially. Suggestions by the German Embassy about the conduct of the trial will be favourably received." France knew that it had to deal with a political hot potato, and Maitre Vincent de Moro-Giafferi (1878-1956), one of the top barristers, was appointed for the defence. Goebbels promptly branded him in the German Press "a defendant of the world Jewish conspiracy." The French kept on delaying the trial.

After the German occupation of France on 15 July 1940, the Gestapo found Grynszpan in a Paris prison and transferred him to the German prison in Berlin-Moabit. A show trial was planned for 16 October 1941. Then a bombshell hit the preparation of the trial. A rumour arose that the true motive of Grynszpan for the killing was his homosexual relationship with vom Rath, whom he had known for some time. The information sheets No.60 from the Minister of Justice to Hitler dated 3

July 1942 reads: "The Jew Grynszpan has admitted in a protocol, that his statement to have had sexual relationships with vom Rath is untrue. He however indicates the suspicion that the murder victim has had homosexual relationships with others. In this respect, it is of interest that the brother of the murdered vom Rath, a Lieutenant Colonel and chief of a cavalry squadron, has been demoted and sentenced to one year imprisonment for homosexual acts."

On receiving this information, Hitler lost his nerve, and ordered the cessation of all further action in this matter until after the final victory. While there are some records of Herschel Grynszpan's further fate, his end is not known. On the 30 November 1960, the District Court of Hannover declared Grynszpan dead as from 8 May1945.

The plan of the Nazis to destroy European Jewry was always part of their program. It is interesting to speculate whether the internal and international intrigues associated with *Kristallnacht* hastened this process, thus preventing many Jews from reaching safety by timely emigration.

The small Jewish-owned shoe store in which my father had worked for nearly two years was destroyed. *Kristallnacht* was followed by the passing of further legislation: Jews were no longer allowed to own or conduct businesses and insurance settlements for the damage done during *Kristallnacht* had to be paid into the government's coffers.

Father was not unemployed for long. On 14 December 1938 he was ordered by the Gestapo to move to Werlte near Hannover to work for the construction company Carl Nicolai. Many German and Austrian Jews worked at that site as forced labourers, building autobahns. His meagre wage did not support our household, so the unstoppable downward slide in our living standards continued.

I was now the man of the house and had to earn my keep. Mother was working all day so, after returning from school, I had to shop, prepare the evening meal, help to clean, do my homework, and learn whatever there was on offer. Social life was on the decline, as everybody was absorbed with their own problems and avoided going out in order to to stay away from molestation and trouble.

Reading, studying and practising the violin were not only a means to an end, but helped me to make my own company sufficiently interesting to be able to live with myself. Mother often unburdened her concerns and told me about the many dramatic events that happened in the Jewish community. We had good communications then and maintained a good rapport with each other for the rest of our lives. Father always kept his worries to himself and he taught me to solve my own problems without bothering others about them. What else could still happen to us after 1938?

We did not have to look for the answer to this question for very long. The year 1939 set us on target towards the Final Solution.

Every Friday night we lift the cup of wine in the circle of our fa Re: newsletter mily and say the traditional Hebrew words: "With this cup we remember the creation of the world and the exodus from Egypt." In the churches, too, each week, a cup of wine is raised, and the priest paraphrases the old Jewish Kiddush doxology with the words: "Do this in memory of Me." How will the Church's Communion Cup "symbolising the blood of the Son of God" who died tragically two thousand years ago, ever accommodate in this cup the blood of the six million sons and daughters of God who died just as tragically in our own time?

The Closed Door

> "Life belongs to the living. He who lives must be prepared for changes." – Johann Wolfgang von Goethe (1749-1832)

The period of making life for the Jews of Germany merely untenable and unsustainable had come to an end with *Kristallnacht.* The laws enacted against Jews by the Third Reich before November 1938 appeared insignificant when compared to what was to follow. The period of destroying our material possessions, our strength and our lives was now followed by a period of liquidating Jewish communal organisations. They were systematically dismantled unless they proved useful to the Gestapo for the winding up of the Jewish presence in Germany.

Hermann Goering had already supported the Nuremberg Laws of 15 September 1935 and he later initiated many economic measures and laws against Jews. On 24 January 1939, Goering issued an order to the Chief of the Security Police Reinhardt Heydrich to proceed with solving the "Jewish Question" through *"emigration and evacuation".* Goebbels and Himmler were far more aggressive and anti-Semitic than Goering, who mainly adopted that attitude because party politics required him to do so.

Goering's deputy, Field Marshal Erhard Milch (1892-1972), was born the son of Anton Milch, a Jewish pharmacist and Clara Milch née Rosenau. Milch was one of the few officers in the German high command of Jewish ancestry. He was investigated by the Gestapo and he got acceptance after Goering stated that Milch's biological father was another man, Karl Brauer. Based on Goering's statement, Milch could receive a "German Blood Certificate" and so avoid further troubles from the Gestapo. Goering's famous quote, *"Wer Jude ist, bestimme ich"* (I decide who is a Jew), is connected to this incident.

In July 1941 Goering issued a memo to Reinhard Heydrich ordering him to organise the practical details of a solution to the "Jewish Question". By the time this letter was written, many Jews had already been killed in Poland,

Russia and elsewhere. At the Wannsee Conference held on 20 January 1942, Heydrich formally announced that genocide of the Jews of Europe was now official Reich policy. Goering did not attend this conference, but he was present at other meetings where the number of people killed was discussed. However, he told the interpreter and psychologist G.M. Gilbert during the Nuremberg Trial that he would never have supported the anti-Jewish measures if he had known what was going to happen. He said: "I only thought we would eliminate Jews from positions in big business and government." In contrast, Goering's younger brother Albert Günther Goering (1896-1966), who saved the lives of Jews during the Holocaust, was considered by Yad Vashem for a Righteous of the Nations Award.

Between 1 January 1939 and the beginning of World War II on 1 September 1939, an estimated further 157,000 Jews left Germany. The door to leave was rapidly closing.

In July 1939, Britain disallowed any further migration of Jews into the British Mandate of Palestine.

In July 1938, F.D. Roosevelt had invited the nations to a conference to deal with the refugee crisis. Switzerland was suggested for the venue, but Switzerland refused to host the conference. Evian in France was finally chosen. The Australian delegation was led by Lieutenant-Colonel Sir Thomas Walter White (1888-1966), Federal Minister for Trade and Customs. White was a good representative of the negative attitude of Australia to the refugee problem. In his speech at the conference he said: "Under the circumstances, Australia cannot do more, for it will be appreciated that in a young country, manpower from the source from which most of its citizens have come, is preferred, while undue privileges cannot be given to one particular class of non-British subjects without injustice to others. It will no doubt be appreciated also, that, as we have no real racial problems, we are not desirous of importing one by encouraging any scheme of large-scale foreign migration."

The USA was generous in accepting affidavits, but the actual intake into the US was slow, as it was regulated by a quota system. The estimated number of Jews trapped in Germany at the outbreak of war was 213,930 of the 500,000 Jews in 1933.

Our family was part of this statistic. In theory, emigration was still possible to neutral countries such as China (Shanghai), Spain and the South Americas. But on 1 October 1941, a law was passed prohibiting Jews from leaving Germany. Germany's attitude to the Jewish problem was changing over time from emigration to extermination. My parents' attitude did not change. They were always optimistic, and no doubt this kept us sane and helped us to adapt to the changing world around us. The year 1939 taught us that the maintenance of our beautiful home and hanging on to our prized possessions became of little importance, compared with staying together, healthy and alive.

Being progressively stripped of our material belongings and having to face up to further laws that prohibited Jews from living in the same apartment buildings and shop for groceries in the same stores as Aryans, helped us to focus on what really mattered in life.

On 22 February 1939, all gold, silver and precious stones had to be handed in. With two washing baskets full of our Sabbath candlesticks, silver cutlery, diamond rings, gold watches and silver ornaments, my mother queued up all day with other Jewish families in front of the City's Public Pawn Office to hand in our belongings, that for years had had pride of place in our home. A small non-itemised receipt was all we received in return. The Nazis made sure to provide the appropriate abuse to the people in the queue by the public.

Little did we know that soon we would be forced to return to hand over our radio. The date of 23 September 1939 was the Jewish Day of Atonement, a date well chosen by the Gestapo for this purpose. On this holiest day of the Jewish religious calendar, Jews were kept standing in the street in the cold autumn weather, thus being prevented from attending the synagogue.

On 23 July 1938, a law had been passed stipulating that Jews had to always carry an Identity Card *(Kennkarte),* and this was followed by a further law on 17 August 1938 that Jews had to have the additional compulsory given name "Israel" for males and "Sarah" for females as from 1 January 1939. I can still hear my parents asking me every time before I left home to go out: "Have you your *Kennkarte* with you, and look after it and don't forget your name is Israel!" I still have my *Kennkarte* with me; however, my name Israel is only one of the many names I have had to adopt to survive in the rough and tumble of life.

Geburtsurkunde

(Standesamt Breslau IV Nr. 827/29

Klaus A u f r i c h t i g

ist am 16. April 1929

in Breslau, Kleiststraße 3 geboren

Vater: Rudolf Aufrichtig, Kaufmann.

Mutter: Elisa Anna Frieda geborene Schneider.

Änderungen der Eintragung: Das Kind führt vom 1.1.1939 ab zusätzlich den jüdischen Vornamen I s r a e l .

Standesamt Breslau IV, den 28. März 1939

Der Standesbeamte

(Siegel)

1326

This amended birth certificate 1 January 1939, recording the additional Jewish first name "Israel".

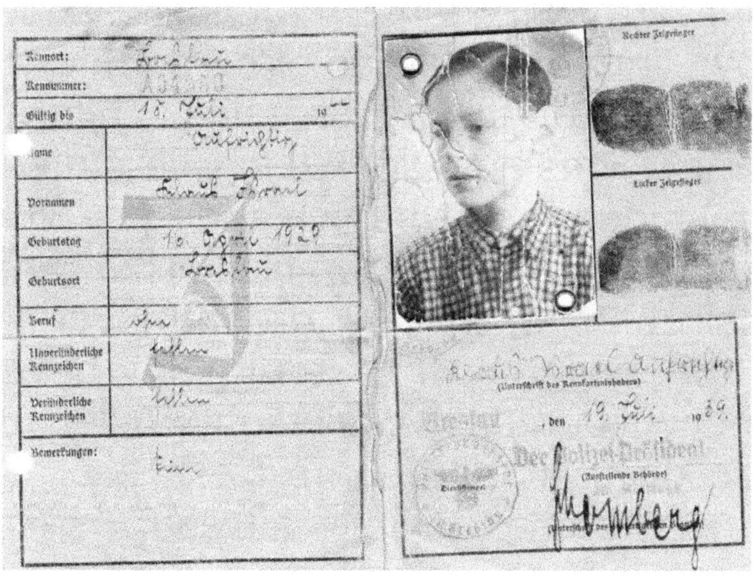

Kennort: Breslau
Kennummer:
Gültig bis 18. Juli 19
Name
Vornamen
Geburtstag
Geburtsort
Beruf
Unveränderliche Kennzeichen
Veränderliche Kennzeichen
Bemerkungen:

Rechter Zeigefinger
Linker Zeigefinger
(Unterschrift des Kennkarteninhabers)
Breslau, den 19. Juli 1939
Der Polizei-Präsident
(Ausstellende Behörde)

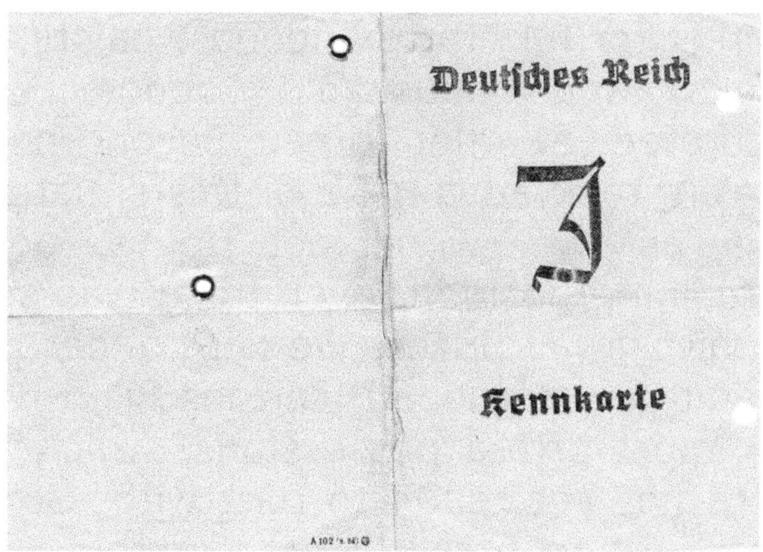

Deutsches Reich
J
Kennkarte

Identification Card to be carried at all times from 19 July 1939.

On 1 September 1939, we had to give up our home in 136

Gabitzstrasse/Adama Prochnika and to move into the caretaker's room in the basement of the Kinderheim (Children's Home) Breslau, der Reichsvereinigung der Juden in Deutschland at 61-65 Gräbschenerstrasse/Grabiszynska. Our small room was below ground level next to the boiler room. It did not have a window, but only a skylight to let in a little daylight and some fresh air.

We had to sell all our excess belongings to reduce the contents of fifteen rooms into one small room. The market for furniture, antiques, paintings, books and household goods was saturated at that time. Second-hand dealers took advantage of this situation, and as we were not in a good bargaining position, everything was sold for give-away prices. We kept under our beds a few cardboard cartons filled with our most prized possessions, which we were not yet ready to part with. So, it was hard to move around in this little room and difficult to clean it properly.

My father was released from the labour camp in the town of Werlte to serve as house-master-educator of the boys, and my mother became the caretaker and kitchen hand in the same Children's Home.

Jewish Children's Home Gräbschenerstrasse 61/65 Breslau/ Wrocław.

In 1874, a medical study of the Jewish community of Prussia was conducted, with the result that in normal times, the average life expectancy between 1800 and 1870 was between 30 and 35 years, and in times of war, famine and widespread epidemics, it was between 25 and 30 years. Of 1000 children, between 250 and 400 died before they reached the age of fourteen. Orphanages were therefore a necessity, and the Breslau

Jewish community had established a great institution in a fine building for this purpose.

On 15 November 1938, a law was passed prohibiting Jewish children from attending schools together with non-Jewish children. This meant that Jewish children living in small communities had to be accommodated in Children's Homes in the larger Jewish communities. The Breslau community had to provide education for the Jewish children from the Province of Silesia and from the Sudetenland.

In July 1939, the Jewish orphanage was transformed into the Children's Home in which we lived, and it became a happy home for over 100 boys and girls, including myself, until 10 September 1940. I slept in our own little room, but otherwise I shared my life with all the other children. We became one happy family. We played football together in the large yard, and protected the little boys and girls from being teased and bullied at school.

We all dreaded having to eat semolina pudding which, due to insufficient kitchen facilities, was usually burnt; it tasted revolting and filled the entire building with the smell of burnt milk. We always looked forward to the rare occasions when the home managed to supply each one of us with half a lemon to dip into sugar and chew as a dessert. The scent from 100 children chewing lemons at the same time filled the building with its aroma. Every child had his or her story to tell.

Little Max Müller had a hydrocephalus, and because of his cuteness and helplessness, he was thoroughly spoilt by everybody.

The boys and girls in the Children's Home in 1940. All these children, with hardly any exceptions, were exterminated during the Holocaust.

The two brothers Hernstädt came from a wealthy and sheltered home in the country. They felt most insecure in the rough and tumble of the Children's Home and so they were mostly holding hands together, protecting one another, a most kind and fragile relationship between these two little boys.

Nelly Schüftan had a Jewish father and a non-Jewish mother. Her father was taken to Buchenwald on 9 November 1938 and when he was released, he was ordered to leave Germany within forty-eight hours. He and his wife went to Palestine, and they left their ten-year-old Nelly behind with her non-Jewish grandparents. The grandparents became concerned about their own future as the persecution of the Jews progressed. They committed Nelly to the Children's Home, thereby sealing Nelly's future fate.

Then there were Werner Tuch and Albert Jacob, who found solace in the teachings and practice of Judaism. They took me under their wing and introduced me to conducting Jewish religious services, and to the wealth of Jewish music and Jewish learning.

One floor of the building housed the remnants of the Jewish Museum with objects of Jewish art from Silesia, going back hundreds of years. The museum was originally part of the city's history museum. These museum rooms, including its historic synagogue, were locked and sealed by the Gestapo on *Kristallnacht.*

Late in 1939, we had a pleasant surprise. The Gestapo took off the seal and confiscated all objects made from precious metal, but we could use the little synagogue again on Friday nights. It was my turn to conduct the Friday night service. It was a special experience to rededicate a beautiful synagogue in a place and at a time when the closure and desecration of synagogues were the order of the day. With hindsight, I deeply regret that I did not pass this privilege on to Werner and Albert, who taught me so much, as neither of them survived the Holocaust.

Going Nowhere

> *"Horresco referens"* Virgil (I shudder to recall it) – Publius Vergilius Maro (70-19 BCE)

I went to the *Private Vorschule-Gertrud Wohl* for the four years of primary school required for being eligible to enter high school. After *Kristallnacht* on 9 November 1938 the Gertrud Wohl school had to close for many reasons. With the blocking of bank accounts, Jews could no longer afford the fees; the non-Jewish teachers were prevented from teaching and mixing with Jews; two of the Jewish teachers had not survived the deportation after *Kristallnacht,* and Jews were no longer allowed to conduct a school in a building that also had non-Jewish tenants. All private Jewish schools were closed and there was only one very large Jewish school left.

I had to transfer to the *Private Jüdische Volksschule zu Breslau* in the *Rhediger Schule,* located in at Rhedigerplatz 3. I completed my primary schooling in April 1939, then until 9 April 1941, I attended the *Private Jüdische höhere Schule* with the aim of getting the final certificate, the *Arbitur* that entitles entry to university.

After my sheltered school days in the posh private school, life in the high school was a culture shock. It had been established to foster Orthodox Judaism and Zionism within its pupils, and was originally called *Private Jüdische Reform-Realgymnasium.* I came from a home with a Liberal Jewish background that believed that being Jewish is a religious and not a racial or national matter. The school was accommodated in a fine building, but it soon became hopelessly overcrowded through the influx of all the children that had been evicted as Jews from non-Jewish schools in the city and the provinces. There were insufficient numbers of Jewish schoolteachers available. Some of our teachers were ex-university lecturers, architects, rabbis and professional musicians.

After Kristallnacht this building at Rhedigerplatz 3 accommodated both the Vorschule (primary school) called Jüdische Volksschule zu Breslau and the Gymnasium (high school) called Jüdische höhere Schule.

I was brought up as "a good little boy". Before long, some roughnecks who enjoyed bullying discovered that I was a softy and I became an easy target for them. Frequently I came home in tears, and although I enjoyed learning, I dreaded having to go to school every morning. My mother would bring me to school and pick me up whenever possible, and well-meaning teachers would admonish the bullies. This of course only exacerbated the situation.

One day my father sat me down, and in a few words explained that in life only I can solve my own problems. His first advice came from his experience as a soldier in World War I: *"Selbst ist der Mann"* (self-reliance and independence makes a man). The second piece of advice was born out of his more recent experience. He taught me that personal possessions and status in life are of a very transient nature, but *Wissen ist Macht* (knowledge is power).

I did solve my problem. When two bullies attacked me again in the schoolyard, I punched them furiously, and as I was always tall and had long arms, they were taken by complete surprise and ended up a mess. They retreated, crying their eyes out as my friends from the Children's Home formed a circle around us and cheered me on. I was never attacked again, and did not require any further help from others. It stopped me also from worrying about them and enabled me to get on with my studies. The few words of Father's advice have helped me to survive against the odds and have served me well for the rest of my life. I still regret that I never reopened this subject with my father to express my gratitude to him.

Shortly thereafter, my newly acquired self-confidence was again put to the test. I received an invitation to report to Gestapo Headquarters in the Breslauer Polizei Präsidium. Justification and details for this directive were not given, and my parents were not allowed to accompany me. Would I come home and would they see me ever again? On arrival at the Gestapo Office, a dozen Jewish boys had joined me. Then the reason for our visit was revealed to us. The Gestapo was moving office from the Breslauer Polizei Präsidium across the road to the administration and school building of the Neue Synagoge, am Anger/Lakowa 8. The synagogue had been destroyed on *Kristallnacht* but the adjoining school and administration building had survived. (It is still in good condition and it now serves as a Polish business college.)

We had been recruited as labourers to shift boxes with files and equipment into the Gestapo's newly requisitioned office building. During this day, an air raid alarm interrupted our work. While the Gestapo officers disappeared into the air-raid shelter, they made us stand in the open, facing the wall of the building with our arms spread out. This prevented us from seeing what was going on and gave us the greatest exposure. We were not aware that at this time, bombers were unlikely to be able to reach Breslau.

Early in 1939, clothing and shoes became rationed. Jews did not get a ration card, but had to apply for a *Bezugsschein* (requisition order), which was not always granted. This created big problems for a fast-growing boy like me. The Jewish community organised a *Kleiderkammer* (clothing exchange) to help solve this problem. There the clothes I had outgrown could be exchanged for someone else's clothes that fitted me. This did not enhance a young boy's image and confidence, but after a while I got used to it, and managed to ignore my somewhat unfashionable appearance.

I acquired a new friend to bring a little life into our dark cellar room. My parents bought me a goldfish on my eleventh birthday. It shared our already overcrowded room, but it was an opportunity for me to derive pleasure from caring for this simple form of life in its goldfish bowl. It is still a reminder of the happy hours I shared with the boys and girls in that home. In May 1942, yet another law was enacted. Jews were no longer allowed to own domestic animals. Is a goldfish a domestic animal? Like the Jews in the Middle Ages who lost every disputation with the Church, it was clear that we would have lost a debate on this question with the Gestapo. The contents of the goldfish bowl were tipped into the toilet and flushed down, to satisfy the new law.

On 4 October 1940, we learnt why the rooms of the Jewish Museum had been unsealed. On the order of the Gestapo, the building had to be vacated within twenty-four hours. The building was required for *Volksdeutsche* – Germans who lived in countries east of the German border and whose home and life were no longer safe since

Hitler's army had occupied these countries.

We were temporarily accommodated in the building of the Gesellschaft der Freunde, in 3/4 Graupenstrasse/Sadowa that had once housed a Jewish Lodge (social club). We slept in the dance hall in this building on newly constructed two-storey bunks fitted with straw paillasses. A dividing wall was erected to separate boys from girls. I fell out of the top bunk bed, landed on my shoulder and smashed my collarbone. An operation to replace it with a metal collarbone was necessary. The 450-bed Jewish hospital had already been confiscated and converted into a German Army hospital. All that was left of the surgical department were a few rooms in a large apartment building in Victoria Strasse/Lwowska.

Again, our stay in this building was short (September to October 1940) as it was required as interim accommodation for the deportation of the older members of the Breslau Jewish community.

Where to go next? The community accommodated us all just for a few days in the most beautiful villa of the Jewish architect Paul Ehrlich (1870-1943), who together with his brother Richard Ehrlich (1866-1942) designed, before 1933, many of the major civic buildings in Breslau. (These two Ehrlich brothers were deported to the KZ *(Konzentrationslager,* concentration camp) Theresienstadt, where both died.) The villa was magnificent, but totally unsuitable for so many people. We all had to sleep on the floor; we could not wash ourselves properly in the one bathroom; we had to live on sandwiches only, as the kitchen facilities were not designed for so many people and we had to queue up to use the only two toilets in the house.

The next move was on 3 October 1940 (until November 1940), to a large Jewish aged-care facility in Kirschallee/Wisniova. The previous residents of this home had been moved into the country transit camps of Grüssau, Tormersdorf and Riebnig, and from there they were all deported between June 1942 and July 1943 to concentration camps for extermination

(1050 to Theresienstadt; 546 to various KZ camps; 97 went to Auschwitz and 107 died in the three transit camps). This old-age home was infested with bed bugs, and it was hard to sleep at night as we were bitten and had to scratch ourselves to get some relief. Room by room the place was fumigated against the bed bugs. This building was also confiscated, and we were on the move again. Another temporary solution had to be found.

After my release from hospital I did not rejoin the children, as meanwhile the Children's Home had been moved into a manor house outside the city. From there the children were deported in February 1943 into an extermination camp. My father cared for them until April 1941, but we moved in November 1940 into a single room of a two-room apartment in a *Judenhaus* at 65 Kopischstrasse/Stalowa. The children never returned and never grew old. I can still hear their laughter and treasure their friendship, and I am grateful for having shared with them, some of the days of our lives.

The year 1940 still brought a foretaste of things to come. In February, the first deportations of German Jews took place. The Jews of Schneidemühl, Stettin and Stralsund were deported to Lublin. This was followed by 7500 Jews from the German provinces of Baden and the Pfalz being deported to Southern France. Jews were no longer allowed to have a telephone from 29 July 1940. In May 1940, the concentration camp of Auschwitz was established to prepare in earnest for the Final Solution. The knowledge about all these events came to us as rumours, and few were ready to accept these rumours as facts. The wish to stay alive made most shut the facts out of their minds.

The Plot Thickens

> *"Te hominem esse memento."* (Remember that you are a human being.) – A reminder call of the servus publicus to a Roman Triumphant.

In 1939 and 1940, a few non-Jews and Jews still had the courage to have personal relationships with each other. The official record shows that, in those two years, 665 Jews and Christians were sentenced to imprisonment for *Rassenschande* (defilement of the Aryan race). On 20 April 1940, a secret order given by the Supreme Command of the German Wehrmacht was implemented; it expelled non-Jews married to Jews and children of a mixed marriage from the German Army, even if all the members in this marriage belonged to a church.

In June 1941 the plot thickened. Heinrich Himmler ordered Rudolf Höss, the Commander of Auschwitz, to prepare this camp to be a vital link for the Final Solution, through the mass-extermination of Jews. The number crunchers of the Nazi machine had done their homework. They realised that Auschwitz alone could not cope with this job, so in September, Maydanek, and in October, Birkenau opened their doors.

These camps were less than 300 kilometres away from Breslau, but at the time they were of no concern to us. We had more immediate problems to deal with. We were prohibited from using public telephones (29 July 1940), and were not allowed to have private telephones. We could no longer use public transport without the express permission of the Gestapo (1 May 1942), and this permission was only granted to travel to and from work, provided the place of work was, in the opinion of the authorities, far enough away from home. We were not allowed to leave our home after 9pm in summer and 8pm in winter (1 September 1939).

My father had to leave his job in the Children's Home and work as a labourer in the local paper-mill in Sacrau near Breslau. My mother had to wash the city's tramcars all night and work as a forced labourer in the FAMO factory *(Fahrzeug- und Motoren- Werke* – Automobile and Engine Works), a German vehicle manufacturer in the early twentieth century.)

The following is the English translation of a letter the children of the Home gave my father when he had to leave them. The letter acknowledges that my father was a very special person, but in addition it expresses the anxiety of these children who were cut off from their parents and their homes and who were in urgent need of care and support. Their ages ranged from six to fourteen years. All of them were deported from Breslau on 3 May 1942 to Izbica with a transport of approximately 1,000 Jewish people. Some were redistributed from this camp to the concentration camps of Sobibor, Belzec and Majdanek, but all of them were gassed and cremated.

Breslau, 30 April 1941

Dear Mr Aufrichtig!

A long time; months after months have elapsed, during which you have lovingly cared for us.

We always felt that you were closer to us than was required by your job.

Your loving care for us is unforgettable!

We want our close friendship to continue, even though circumstances force you to leave us.

Your advice and teaching was always practical and educational and it will remain with us forever and help us in our future lives.

Your compassion with our childhood suffering was the best indication of our close relationship.

You never failed to give us practical advice when we needed help. Your kind and fatherly care will remain within our hearts.

Words fail us to express our gratitude to you!

We wish you and your family good health and the opportunity to stay together.

These are our wishes which will always be in our thoughts and hearts.

Your

Young Friends.

The *Private Jüdische höhere Schule* was closed by the Gestapo on 9 April 1941 as Jews were no longer allowed access to higher education, however, Jewish children still had to go to school. Consequently, I had to go back to the *Private Jűdische Volksschule zu Breslau* on 9 April 1941. I stayed at this school until 30 June 1942 when the law was passed that prohibited Jews from having any kind of school education.

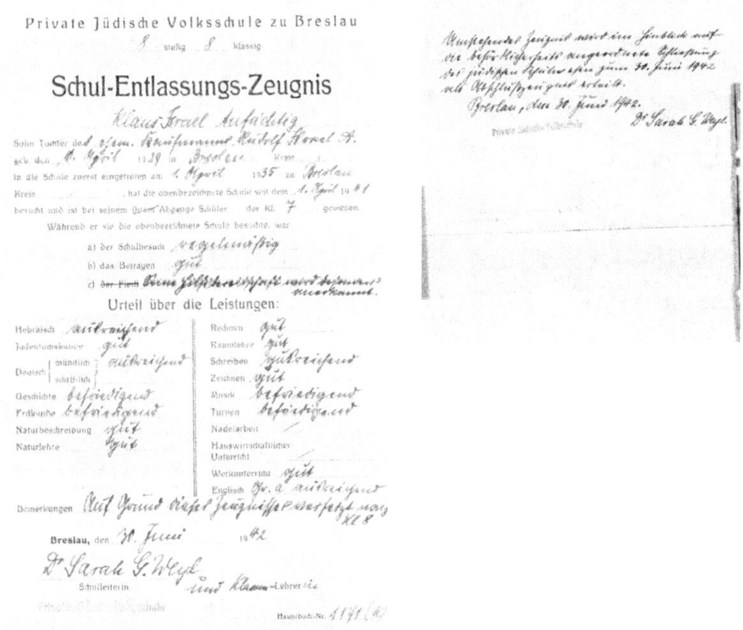

Private Jüdische Volksschule zu Breslau

8 stufig 8 klassig

Schul-Entlassungs-Zeugnis

Klaus Israel Aufrichtig

Sohn ~~Tochter~~ des Kaufmanns Rudolf Israel A.

geb. den 1. April 1929 in Breslau Kreis

in die Schule zuerst eingetreten am 1. April 1935 zu Breslau

Kreis .... hat die obenbezeichnete Schule seit dem 1. April 1941

besucht und ist bei seinem ~~ihrem~~ Abgange Schüler der Kl. 7 gewesen.

Während er sie die obenbezeichnete Schule besuchte, war

a) der Schulbesuch regelmäßig

b) das Betragen gut

c) ~~der Fleiß~~

Urteil über die Leistungen:

Hebräisch ausreichend	Rechnen gut
Judentumskunde gut	Raumlehre gut
Deutsch mündlich / schriftlich ausreichend	Schreiben gut ausreichend
	Zeichnen gut
Geschichte befriedigend	Musik befriedigend
Erdkunde befriedigend	Turnen befriedigend
Naturbeschreibung gut	Nadelarbeit —
Naturlehre gut	Hauswirtschaftlicher Unterricht —
	Werkunterricht gut
	Englisch ausreichend

Bemerkungen

Breslau, den 30. Juni 1942

Dr Sarah G. Weyl

Schulleiterin

und Klassen-Lehrerin

Hauptbuch-Nr. 1141

Breslau, den 30. Juni 1942.

Dr Sarah G. Weyl.

From 30 June 1942 Jewish children were longer allowed to go to school. The note on the reverse side of my final Primary School Certificate confirms this government regulation.

We were fortunate that a very nice Jewish family who had one young son occupied the other room of our two-room apartment in Kopischstrasse 65. We had known the Korngrün family for a long time, as they did not live far from our large apartment which we had to abandon when we moved into the Children's Home. Furthermore, Mr Korngrün was a commercial agent who used to call on my grandfather's business to sell him his wares.

From Thursday, 19 September 1941 onwards we had to wear the Yellow Star of David. It was issued to us on 1 September 1941 against signing the following receipt: "I acknowledge the receipt of one *Judenstern* (Jewstar). I am aware of all my legal obligations on the wearing of the Jew-star and about the prohibition to wear any Orders and Medals. I also understand that I am not allowed to leave my place of residence without the written permission of the local police. I undertake to treat this sign of identification with care and when sewing it on to my outer garment to fold over the excess material. I further acknowledge receipt of a copy of the above." The bottom of the receipt read: "Neglect will be punished with a fine of 150 German marks or six weeks imprisonment. Security laws allowing for more severe sentences remain unaffected."

This is the Star of David I had to wear from 1 September 1941.

On Friday, 20 September 1941 the Sabbath service was crowded. The many yellow stars adorned the assembled crowd and left no doubt as to our Jewish identity. A few days later the non-Jewish shopkeeper told my mother he was rather surprised that I seemed to wear the star like a badge of honour. I think I was no exception – we all did.

It was a dark and dreary September morning in 1941 when, between 6 and 7am, a hammering of fists on the entrance door woke us up. "Open up, Gestapo!" My mother opened the door. Two Gestapo officers pushed her aside. "Where are the Jews Korngrün?" They opened the door of the room the family Korngrün occupied, without knocking. The family was still in bed. We were ordered to stay in our room. The Korngrüns had to get dressed immediately, pack some essentials, but not more than they could carry, take bread along for a two-day journey, and leave their tools in the entrance hall (sewing machine, axe, hammer, screwdrivers, bucket, etc.). Mrs Korngrün was expected to dress herself in the presence of the Gestapo officers. She still had the courage to throw them out of the room for a few minutes. The family was not allowed to lock the toilet door, but only keep it ajar.

The Gestapo then sealed their room. They were told that they would be resettled in the newly acquired Eastern Territories of Germany the *General Gouvernement,* so that they, at long last, would have "the opportunity to do an honest day's work". Their tools would be collected later, and the contents of their room would be sent to them in due course. It was not an implausible story, as some elderly Breslau Jews had already been moved into transit camps in the close-by country areas of Tormersdorf, Grüssau and Riebnik, and they did write to relatives and friends now and again.

I had to accompany the Korngrüns to help carry their luggage. By tram under Gestapo guard, we went to the Schiesswerdersaal, a local dance hall, where already many Jewish families were assembled, and most of them sat on their rucksacks and suitcases, waiting to move on. The Korngrüns seemed to be a little more at ease meeting so many fellow Jews.

Their six-year-old son Heini cried inconsolably. His teddy bear had been left behind. His mother begged me to get it so that she could comfort Heini on the journey ahead. I went back home, and found the teddy still lying in the hall. I went back again to the Schiesswerdersaal, and what a joy it was for the child to be reunited with his teddy bear and to find comfort from it.

The tools were never collected. Gestapo records show that the transport left Breslau on Friday, 21 November 1941. It was destined for Riga. However, it was intercepted on Tuesday, 25 November 1941 in Kaunas, and 693 men, 1155 women and 152 children, a total of 2000 Breslau Jews were shot in this city on that day. Maybe the teddy bear was of some comfort, before a bullet ended Heini Korngrün's young life.

On 3 April 1942, the law about the wearing of the yellow star was supplemented with the following regulation: "Jews who have to wear the *Judenstern* have to mark their dwellings as follows. The dwelling must be marked with a *Judenstern* (black print on white paper) similar in size and design to the identification to be worn on the clothing. This mark of identification is to be glued on to the outside of the door frame to the entrance of the dwelling."

The people in this photo were all shot 48 hours later in Kaunas, Lithuania on 25 November 1941 (693 men, 1155 women, 152 children). Helmut Eschwege Kennzeichen Berlin 1981

Der Befehlshaber der Sicherheitspolizei u. des SD
Einsatzkommando 3

Kauen, am 1.Dezember 1941

Geheime Reichssache!

5 Ausfertigungen!
4. Ausfertigung.

Gesamtaufstellung der im Bereich des EK.3 bis zum 1.Dez.1941 durchgeführten Exekutionen.

Übernahme der sicherheitspolizeilichen Aufgaben in Litauen durch das Einsatzkommando 3 am 2.Juli 1941.
(Das Gebiet Wilna wurde am 9.Aug.41, das Gebiet Schaul[illegible] 2.Okt.41 vom EK.3 übernommen. Wilna wurde bis zu diesem Zei[illegible] vom EK.9 und Schaulen vom EK.2 bearbeitet.)

Auf meine Anordnung und meinen Befehl durch die lit.Partisanen durchgeführten Exekutionen:

4.7.41	Kauen - Fort VII - 416 Juden, 47 Jüdinnen	463
6.7.41	Kauen - Fort VII - Juden	2 514

Nach Aufstellung eines Rollkommandos unter Führung von SS-Ostuf.Hamann und 8 - 10 bewährten Männern des EK.3 wurden nachfolgende Aktionen in Zusammenarbeit mit den lit.Partisanen durchgeführt:

7.41	Mariampole	Juden	32
7.41	"	14 " und 5 komm.Funktionäre	19
.7.41	Girkalinei	komm.Funktionäre	6
[illegible].7.41	Wendziogala	32 Juden, 2 Jüdinnen, 1 Litauerin, 2 lit.Komm., 1 russ.Kommunist	38
9.7.41	Kauen - Fort VII -	21 Juden, 3 Jüdinnen	24
[illegible].7.41	Mariampole	21 " , 1 russ. 9 lit.Komm.	31
[illegible].7.41	Babtei	8 komm.Funktionäre (6 davon Juden)	8
[illegible].7.41	Mariampole	39 Juden, 14 Jüdinnen	53
9.7.41	Kauen - Fort VII -	17 " , 2 " , 4 lit.Komm., 2 komm.Litauerinnen, 1 deutsch.K.	26
[illegible]1.7.41	Panevezys	59 Juden, 11 Jüdinnen, 1 Litauerin, 1 Pole, 22 lit.Komm., 9 russ.Komm.	103
22.7.41	"	1 Jude	1
23.7.41	Kedainiai	83 Juden, 12 Jüdinnen, 14 russ.Komm. 15 lit.Komm., 1 russ.O-Politruk.	125
25.7.41	Mariampole	90 Juden, 13 Jüdinnen	103
28.7.41	Panevezys	234 " , 15 " , 19 russ.Komm., 20 lit.Kommunisten	288
		Übertrag:	3 834

Page 1 of a secret report about the execution of Jews in Kaunas from the Commander of the German Security Police in Kauen (Kaunas), Dr Karl Jäger dated 1 December 1941, saying the executions were carried out by Lithuanian partisan volunteers. Rossijskij Gosudarstvennyj Voennyj Archiv v Moskve

Blatt 5.

-Übertrag: 66 159

Monat Oktober:

Datum	Ort		Anzahl
2.10.41	Zagare	633 Juden, 1107 Jüdinn., 496 J.-Ki. (beim Abführen dieser Juden entstand eine Meuterei, die jedoch sofort niedergeschlagen wurde. Dabei wurden 150 Juden sofort erschossen. 7 Partisanen wurd. verletzt)	2 236
4.10.41	Kauen-F.IX-	315 Juden, 712 Jüdinn., 818 J.-Kind. (Strafaktion weil im Ghetto auf einen deutsch. Polizisten geschossen wurde)	1 845
29.10.41	Kauen-F.IX-	2007 Juden, 2920 Jüdinnen, 4273 Judenkinder (Säuberung des Ghettos von überflüssigen Juden)	9 200

Monat November:

Datum	Ort		Anzahl
3.11.41	Lazdijai	485 Juden, 511 Jüdinn., 539 J.-Kind.	1 535
15.11.41	Wilkowiski	36 " 48 " 31 "	115
25.11.41	Kauen-F.IX-	1159 " 1600 " 175 " (Umsiedler aus Berlin, München u. Frankfurt a.M.)	2 934
29.11.41	" "	693 " 1155 " 152 " (Umsiedler aus Wien u. Breslau)	2 000
29.11.41	" "	17 Juden, 1 Jüdin, die gegen die Ghettogesetze verstossen hatten, 1 R.-Deutscher, der zum jüdischen Glauben übergetreten war und eine Rabinerschule besucht hatte, dann 15 Terroristen der Kalinin-Gruppe	34

Teilkommando des EK.3 in Dünaburg in der Zeit vom 13.7.-21.8.41:

9012 Juden, Jüdinnen und Judenkinder, 573 aktive Kommunisten — 9 585

Teilkommando des EK.3 in Wilna:

Datum	Ort		Anzahl
12.8. bis 1.9.41	Wilna-Stadt	425 Juden, 19 Jüdinnen, 8 Kommunist. 9 Kommunistinnen	461
2.9.41	" "	864 Juden, 2019 Jüdinnen, 817 Judenkinder (Sonderaktion, weil von Juden auf deutsche Soldaten geschossen wurde)	3 700

-Übertrag: 99 804

Page 5 of the same report. The line dated 29.11.41 shows that this transport consisted of 693 men, 1155 women and 152 children, a total of 2000 from Vienna and Breslau. Some of the Breslau people in this transport are shown in the photo on page 77. This transport also included the Korngrün family. The figure bottom right shows a total of 99,804 people were killed by 29 November 1941. Rossijskij Gosudarstvennyj Voennyj Archiv v Moskve

We had to vacate the Kopischstrasse apartment on 10 June 1942, and just two months earlier, the Gestapo collected everything that belonged to the Korngrüns. As always, we were only given 48 hours' notice to vacate. We were moved to Zimmerstrasse/ Joachima Lelewela 5/7 into a four-room apartment with one Jewish family per room, and all of us sharing the small kitchen and bathroom.

It was good to have left Kopischstrasse. After the Korngrüns had been deported, we could not help but keep on looking at the sealed door of their room, thinking of them all the time and wondering what might have become of them. Their pots, plates and spoons left behind in the kitchen were treated by us with utmost respect, as though this would make up for the treatment that was meted out to them.

The owner of the local vegetable store had taken pity on me. I had to do the shopping, as Jews were restricted to shop in designated stores between 4 and 5pm. My parents were still at work at that time of the day, and so it was left to me to queue up and get the little food that was allotted to us on the *Juden Marken* (Jew coupons); these were the same food coupons as were issued to the rest of the population, except that they were overprinted with words *Jude* (Jew) and many of the coupons were overprinted with the word "invalid", thus putting us on a minimum subsistence ration.

On one occasion, the grocer allowed me to call back three times to buy spinach. It took us many hours to process a whole bathtub full of fresh spinach. The great taste of spinach which long ago helped me not to feel hungry for a short time, still lingers on. To run a store for Jews at that time brought the owner extra profit. He filleted the pickled herrings and sold the fillet to his Aryan customers. The non-saleable leftovers he put through the mincer and sold to us Jewish customers. One had gradually learnt to eat anything if it stopped the feeling of being hungry.

In retrospect, the increased everyday chores and worries kept us sane, as they left little time for brooding and focusing on the real issues before us.

The Unfolding of the Plan

> "Truth will come to light; murder cannot be hid long." – William Shakespeare (1564-1616), *Merchant of Venice*

The year 1942 was the real *annus horribilis.* The first transport "East" in 1941 of 2,000 people was just a pilot operation. In 1942 most the Breslau Jewish community was deported: 1,000 people on 3 May 1942; 1,100 people on 27 July 1942; 1,065 people on 31 August 1942. The year 1943 was the year of clean-up operations. People who were still required in the local essential industry were gradually replaced and deported: 102 persons on 24 February 1943; more than 200 on 5 March 1943; 277 on 2 April 1943; 39 on 9 June 1943; 161 on 11 June 1943; 18 on 16 June 1943; more than 60 on 27 October 1943. The obvious fact that Germany was losing the war did not stop the deportations from Breslau in 1944. Seventy-three persons were deported on 9 January 1944; three on 11 January 1944; eighteen on 25 April 1944 and the last person was deported on 8 November 1944. These figures add up to 6,117 people being sent to concentration camps to be exterminated from just the one Jewish community of Breslau.

The rabbi of the community was given the number of people to be deported for each transport by the Gestapo. The selection criteria were: first the rich to enable the State to take over their frozen property, followed by those unable to work and dependent on social services, and thereafter those working in essential heavy industry whenever they could be replaced with Aryan workers. Then, it was the turn of *Frontkämpfer* (returned and decorated soldiers of World War I) and finally Jews living in a mixed marriage, and *Geltungsjuden* (the offspring of a mixed marriage where all the members of the marriage had adhered to the Jewish religion). There was the constant fear, will we be next?

Baden-Baden Jewish men rounded up for incarceration in the Buchenwald concentration camp. Stadtarchiv Baden-Baden

The will to survive gave us selective understanding of the facts. One day my father came home from work in a state of utter agitation. An SS officer had tackled him in the street, saying: *"Du lebst noch Jude! Dir werden wir schon bald einen Genickschuss geben!"* (You are still alive, Jew! We will soon arrange a shot into the back of your skull for you.) I believe my father was upset about the callousness of the man and Father's inability to defend himself there. I do not think it would have occurred to my father that this threat was based on what happened. The lack of reliable information, the existence of so many conflicting rumours and the unwillingness to accept these rumours as truth, left most Jews with a strong mental constitution. There was always the hope for liberation without speculating about the nature of possible future torment.

We did hear rumours about the *Wannseekonferenz* (Wannsee Conference) of 20 January 1942, and that it had decided on the industrial extermination of European Jews, but their official resolution sounded more reassuring; it read: "Under appropriate supervision, as part of the Final Solution, Jews shall be used, in a suitable manner, as workers in the Eastern Territories ... A considerable number of them will, without doubt, be lost through natural depletion." Much more troubling to us was the news that on 6 March 1942, the Conference of eleven Cabinet Ministers had decided that issue of mixed marriage had to be sterilised and mixed marriages had to be divorced by law. However, the implementation of this decision was postponed.

Once again, the many little irritations of life prevented us from brooding over the larger issues. In January, we had to hand in furs and woollen garments; on 9 and 18 June 1942 all surplus items of clothing, bicycles, optical apparatus, typewriters and gramophone records were confiscated; on 19 October 1942 coupons for milk, meat, and wheat-based products were cancelled on our ration cards.

From 17 March 1942, another extermination camp was required, and so Belzec was a new place to worry about. From 22 April 1942 Jews were no longer allowed to go to Aryan hairdressers. The few Jews able to cut one's hair short without necessarily making it look attractive, had to fill the gap. It was a blessing in disguise, as the Jewish hairdressers' rooms became a clearing house for information and rumours.

On 30 July 1942, all remaining religious objects made from precious metals had to be handed over. At religious services, the silver ornaments on the Torah scroll disappeared and the silver wine goblet was replaced by a simple glass. On 1 July 1942, Jews were no longer allowed to go to school and from 9 October 1942 Jews were no longer allowed to buy books. All Jewish schools were thus closed. It did not take the Gestapo very long to conclude that Jewish children, regardless of age, should be enlisted to do forced labour, so from the end of July 1942, I started work in the chemical factory Charles Böger & Co. My tiny income was taxed with an additional 15 per cent *Juden Sondersteuer* (Tax Penalty for Jews) in addition to normal income tax.

The period between school being prohibited for Jewish children, and forced labour, presented a problem for Jewish parents and for the Jewish community. Adult supervision was not available, and children were either left alone at home or free to roam the streets, getting up to the usual pranks children do. These pranks could prove life-threatening to them, should the police or Gestapo charge them for misdemeanours. The community tried to solve this problem by locking children up and making us work in the large historic cemetery of the Breslau Jewish community in Lohestrasse. The cemetery was surrounded by a high wall, and lockable with high wrought-iron gates.

It used to be well cared for in the past, and its old trees made it look from the outside like a beautiful private park. It had a personal interest for me, as I could give my special attention to the graves of my great-grandparents, the three brothers of my father who were buried there, and our famous distant relative Friederike Kempner, whose unusual poetry earned her the name the *Schlesische Nachtigal* (Silesian Nightingale). Friederike fought for many causes in her time, one of them was cremation, and she was one of the first people to be cremated in modern German society. The great German theatre critic and writer, Alfred Kempner, changed his name to Alfred Kerr so as not to be associated with his flamboyant relative Friederike. To work in this cemetery was like taking lessons in history.

There was the oldest Breslau tombstone of "Rabbi David of a nice voice, son of Rabbi Sar Shalom (Prince of Peace)" who died on 4 August 1203, a cantor of the Breslau religious congregation.

The grave of one of the founders of the labour movement in Europe, Ferdinand Lassalle, was visited by crowds of workers for each May Day celebration before 1933. He died in a pistol duel on 31 August 1864 in Switzerland, to which he was challenged as a consequence of his love for a non-Jewish girl belonging to the Silesian aristocracy called Helene von Doenniges.

The graves of the historian Professor Heinrich Graetz, the compiler of the first methodical modern Jewish history, and his wife Marie Graetz, the aunt of Sir John Monash, were not far from the grave of the family Milch, whose descendant Field Marshall Erhard Milch worked closely together with Hitler's ministerial friends Albert Speer and Reichsmarschall Hermann Goering for Germany's final victory, despite his Jewish ancestry.

A little further away was the burial place of the family of Edith Stein, the Jewish seeker who ended up as the

Carmelite nun, Theresa Benedicta vom Kreuz[1]. Her plea to Pope Pius XII to intervene for her fellow Jews remained

1 Edith Stein was born on 12 October 1891 (Yom Kippur) in Breslau into an Orthodox Jewish household. Edith later became an atheist, before being baptised into the Roman Catholic Church on 1 January 1922. Edith finally became a Catholic nun. She died on 9 August 1942 in Auschwitz. She was a German philosopher educated by the Albert Ludwig University of Freiburg, the University of Breslau (Wrocław) and the University of Göttingen. Her sister Rosa Stein also converted to Christianity. The Reichskommissar of the Netherlands, Arthur Seyss-Inquart, ordered the arrest of all Jewish converts who had previously been spared. Along with 243 baptised Jews living in the Netherlands, Stein was arrested by the SS on 2 August 1942. Stein and her sister Rosa were imprisoned in the concentration camps of Amersfoort and Westerbork, before being deported to Auschwitz where they died. She was made a saint by the Catholic Church. Pope John Paul II canonised her on 11 October 1998, as St Teresa Benedicta of the Cross. It was said during the ceremony that "She was a seeker of truth in various religions and philosophies".

unanswered. Not only her fellow Jews, but Edith herself ended up in Auschwitz. Maybe, at times, the power structure of the Church takes precedence over the humble quotation of its founder from the Torah: "To love your neighbour."

A change of plan took place. The Gestapo ordered the Jewish community to move us from the historical cemetery in Lohestrasse, to the newer and much larger one in Cosel. It was a mismatch, as the number of young people available had declined through deportation and through being drafted to do forced labour. At the same time the workload was increased, as the area of this cemetery was vast. The bronze doors of family vaults and the steel surrounds of some of the more elaborate graves had been dismantled, and this metal was used for the war effort. There was a hidden agenda for our transfer.

The community received regular deliveries of bodies for burial and we had to help dig graves. The bodies came from the nearby labour camps of Hundsfeld, Masselwitz, Breslau-Neukirch and Klettendorf for Jews from the Polish part of Upper Silesia. These people were not shot or gassed, but were merely worked to death. A 1990 study by Daniel Bogacz of the University of Breslau (Wrocław) indicates that 122 Jews died in these camps. It was food for thought! What was our future? One could not imagine the extent of industrial destruction of human life, but this event certainly raised our fears and concerns to a far higher level of awareness.

Moving from place to place and living close together with so many people during the Hitler years gave rise to some very special and enduring friendships. One of our dear friends was Miss Ottilie Schein, who had been assigned to us as a sub-tenant as far back as 1934 while we were still living in our original apartment. We visited one another as often as possible over the years and always kept in touch. She was a teacher of English, French and Spanish, a very much sought after profession during the Hitler years, in a Jewish community where everyone was desperately trying to emigrate.

In May 1942 she visited us to let us know, with tears running down her cheeks, that her gifted young pupil Anita Treitel had committed suicide (16 November 1941) to avoid further persecution. Then she showed us her own order to report for deportation on the following day.

She confessed that she had not banked all the money she had received for her language lessons, and she thought this money might help her to buy some things at the destination of her journey. How could she take the money along safely? She owned a very small feather cushion. My mother and she rolled the bank notes into little cotton balls, put these balls into the cushion, and then sewed the cushion up again. The unforgettable sight of the two women sitting in Ottilie's sparsely furnished room, covered with white feathers that were flying around everywhere, will always stay in my memory. Miss Schein had only one kidney; the other had been removed by surgery, and she was quite meticulous about drinking appropriate health teas at regular intervals. And there I had to help and go to many chemists and buy a large quantity of her health teas, just in case they would not be readily obtainable on the journey. When we said our final goodbye, she had nothing to worry about. Her few belongings were well packed, her money was safely hidden, and she had enough tea for the journey. Little did she know that all her worries would be over for all time after her arrival in concentration camp.

Not only friends, but also family disappeared from our sight. One of my father's cousins, Walter Schimmelburg, was still able to send us a Red Cross card from the Warsaw Ghetto stating that he and his wife Fanny Schimmelburg were well. He probably did not know when he wrote this card that only days later their lives would be ended.

Another cousin, Ellie Ritter, left Breslau for Theresienstadt. When visiting Theresienstadt in 1993, I found the following record: "Ellie Ritter deported to Theresienstadt with transport IX/4 from Breslau on 2.4.1943, personal transport number 197; transported from Theresienstadt to Auschwitz on

23.10.1944, personal transport number 1005." Ellie was widowed and a very wealthy lady. In 1936, she had packed many containers with her belongings and had them stored in Hamburg, hoping that Hitler would be a passing phase in German history, and that she could retrieve and unpack these containers in her home again after Hitler's demise. If necessary, however, she was ready to send them to the USA and join one of her sons in Baltimore who had not played such high stakes as his mother, and who had emigrated to the USA in time. Ellie's timing was out, and she was trapped in Germany. She was called up to leave Breslau with the first transport in November 1941. She never gave up easily and she accidentally-deliberately fell and broke her hip, which landed her in the Jewish hospital to have her hip repaired by her surgeon friend Dr Siegmund Hadda. Every time a transport left Breslau, Ellie arranged for yet another hip operation that made her immobile again until she finally had to leave with one of the last transports. It is sad that her fighting spirit failed to save her life. Aunt Ellie's transport must have been the last of eleven transports sent from Theresienstadt to Auschwitz between September and October 1944. She missed the end of the war by a mere six months.

The last member of our family to leave Breslau was my grandmother's sister, Meta Bernstein, to me just "Tante Meta". She was an unworldly, kind-hearted old lady, who was always heavily relying on us to help her with her problems. After moving from one aged home to another, she ended up in one of the few rooms kept for the aged by the remnants of the Jewish Breslau community. In August 1942, the residents of this aged home had to board buses for deportation to Theresienstadt. We packed Meta's belongings, but we could not persuade her to dress suitably and practically for the journey. She dressed in her best, looking as though she was going to an afternoon coffee party with her friends, just like in the good old days. She wore a necklace that got tangled with the strap of her shoulder bag. It broke, and all the beads scattered throughout the bus. She tried to pick them up and she thereby delayed the boarding of the bus for her fellow travellers. A Gestapo man shouted at her, grabbed her by the arms and threw her into the bus seat. We were not allowed on the bus to calm her. We waited for her to leave. Tears were streaming down her face when we caught sight of her as the bus went past.

The following is the only memorial of her in the record books of the concentration camp of Theresienstadt: "Meta Bernstein, deported to Theresienstadt with transport 11-2 from Breslau on 31.8.1942, personal transport number 904, died in Theresienstadt on 29.10.1942." Although she was in good physical condition when she left Breslau, she lived for only 59 days in Theresienstadt.

During the first four months of the Theresienstadt Ghetto the dead were buried, but as the mortality rate increased, and a total of 33,000 people died in this camp, the dead were later cremated and the ashes were placed into paper urns and stored in a columbarium. With the end of the war approaching, the Nazis tried to conceal the Theresienstadt atrocities. In November 1944, they ordered the prisoners to dump all the stored ashes into the river Eger, a job that took four days. Thus, this river became Aunt Meta's final resting place.

In November and December of that year, the Allied troops landed in North Africa, the Russians attempted a counteroffensive, and the Allied nations promised to revenge the actions against the Jews. All this was cold comfort to us, as it was an incentive for the Nazis to accelerate their program and to achieve the Final Solution.

Watching and Waiting

> *"Ôte-toi de là, que je m'y mette."* (Get out of the way, so I can take your place.) – Saint-Simon, Compte de Claude Henri de Rouvroy (1760-1825)

We watched the happenings in the world with both great hope and apprehension. Was there an end to our suffering in sight, and if so, would we last the distance? The following describes the situation in 1943:

Stalingrad had surrendered; the army officers of the German Heeresgruppe Mitte attempted to assassinate Hitler; the last German and Italian forces had surrendered in Africa; the Allied Army had landed in Sicily; Italy had surrendered to the Allies and had declared war on Germany; Jews had mounted resistance in the Warsaw Ghetto and in the concentration camps of Treblinka and Sobibor, and the first trial against German war criminals took place in Charkow.

Heinrich Himmler ordered all ghettos to be closed and the Jewish prisoners to be transferred to extermination camps; the *Reichsvereinigung der Juden in Deutschland* (Representative Organisation of German Jews) was liquidated; Jews lost the protection of the German courts but they became subject to police action; all Jews who had been imprisoned were transferred to concentration camps for life, after having served their prison sentence regardless of the reason for or the length of the sentence; and last but not least the installation of gas chambers using Cyclon B gas was introduced into many camps.

All these dramatic events hardly impacted upon the life of our immediate family. Many of them passed us by, unnoticed.

Zimmerstrasse/Joachima Lelewela 5/7 was our penultimate home in Breslau before deportation. In 1943, many of the houses in this short street were *Judenhäuser* (houses for Jews only). We lived in a five-room apartment, and every room was occupied by one family. Our next-room tenant was a locksmith, Mr Armer, who was still allowed to work in one room to fix any metalwork problems for the few remaining Jews. Whenever possible he would take me along to his workshop, treating me like an apprentice, and teaching me the art of making keys, fixing locks and welding.

My father did not encourage it, as in the evening after work, he taught me Latin, Greek, French, history, etc., and he expected me to do my homework during the day. I also had to visit a mathematician, Dr Blumenthal, who gave me lessons in return for me doing his shopping.

In the little spare time left, I found refuge in music. For some years, I had already learnt the violin from Konzertmeister Siegfried Rosenthal, the one-time concertmaster of the Breslau Opera House and the Silesian Philharmonic Orchestra. He lived opposite us in Zimmerstrasse. As always, I went in the evening for my lesson to study the beautiful Violin Concerto in A minor by J.S. Bach.

This time the lesson was interrupted by an unexpected visit from Elfriede

Breslauer. Before the persecution of the Jews, Elfriede was the leader of the second violins in the Silesian Philharmonic Orchestra. She had always been a good friend of the Rosenthals. She was agitated, and showed Siegfried and his wife a letter. They embraced and cried in one another's arms. My lesson was terminated, but I could stay and listen to Siegfried and Elfriede, accompanied by Siegfried's wife at the piano, play Bach's Concerto for Two Violins in D minor. The classical majesty of the beautiful middle movement *largo ma non tanto* became a prayer. The letter Elfriede had shown to Siegfried was her order to report to the Freundesaal on the following day for deportation to Auschwitz. (For many years, the Freundesaal had been the ballroom of a Jewish club *Gesellschaft der Freunde* that had seen countless great celebrations in happier days. It now served as the assembly point for the Breslau Jews to be transported to the various extermination camps.) Elfriede never returned from this journey.

Many old people still lived in their own room, in buildings that once belonged to the Jewish community. Most of them could no longer manage their affairs, and we, the ex-school boys, had to bring food for them every day from the community kitchen, until we too were drafted to do forced labour. This kitchen was established by the Breslau Jewish community in the Freundesaal, where the deportees had to be housed and fed for 48 hours until they were taken by bus to the railway station for their final journey. In between transports, the kitchen in this building was available to cook for the elderly and infirm of the community.

I called daily on the one-time conductor of the choir of the Neue Synagoge, Mr Benjamin (Benno) Pulvermacher and his wife, a mezzo-soprano of note, performing under the stage name Jettka Finkenstein. They were a dear old couple in their late seventies. Their tiny room was decorated with photos, certificates and trophies of their once most successful musical careers. One day, Mr Pulvermacher gave me a few bank notes, expressed his heartfelt thanks to me for my help and wished me all the best for the future. I did not want to take the money. No one had anything to give away.

He insisted. When I returned the next day with their food, the door to their room was wide open. Neighbours were cleaning out their prized memorabilia and putting them into rubbish bins. They were surprised that I had not been told that the couple had committed suicide by opening the gas tap in their room the night before. It all happened on 26 August 1942. I can still see before my eyes these two kindly old people waiting for me every day, their only visitor to arrive with their food. I returned the two spare meals to the communal kitchen. I was asked: "Why didn't you eat the food? It's cold now." I was hungry, but I was not yet ready for such great pragmatism.

Notices were regularly sent ordering members of the Breslau Jewish community to report for deportation to the Freundesaal. The perception that the Gestapo provided the communal leadership with only the required numbers to be deported, but left it to the rabbis to fill in the names and deliver the notices to the individuals and families, was widespread.

I recall good friends of Rabbi Reinhold Lewin feeling very bitter and let down by him, when they were notified to join one of the early transports. There were some compassionate managers of Breslau German firms who applied to the Gestapo, claiming that Jews working for them were indispensable for the war effort. It may have helped one or another for a while, but in the final analysis, it was only a matter of delaying the inevitable. The last rabbi of Breslau, Dr Reinhold Lewin and his family were themselves deported in the end. A story was told that the rabbi, his wife, his young daughter and teenage son, were given the choice by the Gestapo, for a job well done, between deportation to either Theresienstadt or Auschwitz. Rabbi Lewin was reported to have replied: *"Ich gehe mit meiner Gemeinde mit."* (I go together with my community.) He consequently shared the fate of his community in Auschwitz.

Rabbi Dr Reinhold Lewin, his wife Eva and their son Ulli.

Ordner (orderlies) were trained to assist the deportees with the repacking of their luggage and to eliminate any excess they could not carry. The elderly were recalled from nearby transit camps to join those who had still remained in Breslau for the final journey. Jews who still lived in country towns had to join the members of the Breslau community, after being temporarily accommodated in the Freundesaal. We, the older schoolboys, had to help. We prepared bunks, carried luggage, dished out food, and helped the deportees to board the bus or train for their final journey. We did not know their destination at the time, but the treatment meted out to them by Gestapo officers did not inculcate confidence.

Sodium cyanide and cooking gas was always an option to avoid the journey. A study of the Berlin Jewish community in 1943 revealed that 25.2 per cent of all deaths reported at that time were suicide. Daniel Bogacz, in the journal of the University of Wrocław (Breslau) of 1990, analysed the corresponding Breslau statistics with the following results: most of the persons who committed suicide were women over 50 years old, who came from the middle-class, and used chemicals for this purpose. More than half of them died in the Jewish hospital, and the question arises, did the medical staff of the hospital allow matters to proceed in accordance with the patients' wishes. Bogacz concluded that the reasons for Jewish self-destruction are of a complex nature and mainly rooted in the psyche of the individual. Rationalisation and generalisation are not possible.

I remember the bodies of Arnold Berger, the Neue Synagoge organist, his wife Alice Helene and their children, Arthur and Marianne Eva Gerda, lying dead in the middle of the hall after having taken cyanide. A whole family joined in death. The recorded date of this event is 29 February 1943.

My father's best friend, Erich Silbermann, and his wife were special people for me. They were both deaf and dumb. Erich had made a great career for himself by being one of the city's top photographers, and many of his photos are still witness to Breslau's history. He was also an inventor and as he was totally deaf he had designed an alarm clock that would release a heavy steel ball and would wake him up when the ball shook his bed. His doorbell would also release a ball that was suspended from the ceiling and swing across the room when the bell button was pressed. These were great toys for me to play with whenever we visited them. One evening in 1943, Erich and his wife came to say goodbye to all of us before they had to report for deportation. They never went on this journey. We knew that it was their final goodbye.

Life is a prison with open doors, but not many have the courage to exit through these doors in their own time. The morality of Jews assisting the murder of Jews by the Nazis by committing suicide has often been questioned. I believe only those who have lived as victims through the Holocaust are entitled to make a comment on this question and I doubt that many will exercise this right.

Moving On

> *"Dies irae, dies illa, solvet saeclum in favilla."* (Day of wrath, day of terror, that day will dissolve the world into ashes.) – Thomas of Celano (1200-65 CE)

Life in the year 1943 had been most depressing, and life in 1944 was even worse, as the Jewish world around us was disintegrating. The official count of Jews by the Gestapo on 1 September 1944 stated that there were only 15,574 Jews left in Germany of the 500,000 Jews (1933).

On 6 June 1944, the Allied Forces had landed in Normandy and on 20 July we were elated to hear that Hitler had been assassinated in his military headquarters, only having to learn hours later that he had survived the coup. Hitler claimed that his survival was due to the *g öttliche Vorsehung* (divine providence) and that this providence gave him the right to murder the conspirators, together with their families. The Third Reich was crumbling, but this did not happen quickly enough for us, as it had hardly any immediate beneficial effect on our lives. The constant fear of becoming a direct target of the Final Solution; the hard-forced-labour combined with a harsh home environment and feeling hungry and cold most of the time, made it most difficult to focus on the rigid program of home education that my father had devised for me.

The last cultural event of the *Jüdischer Kulturbund* had taken place in October 1941 in the previously mentioned Freundesaal. This Jewish Cultural Association was established in August 1933, in anticipation of the Nazi government establishing the *Reichskulturkammer* (Chamber of Culture of the Third Reich) on 22 September 1933. Jews were excluded from membership and only members of the Chamber could practise the arts in Germany. Furthermore, a law was enacted on 6 December 1938 which prohibited Jews from visiting theatres, cinemas, cabarets, concerts, libraries, museums, exhibitions, entertainment venues, sports venues and swimming pools. The *Kulturbund* managed two symphony orchestras, one opera company, three theatre groups, several choirs, chamber music ensembles and it organised films and lectures, employing 2500 German Jewish artists, who were no longer allowed to perform in German theatres and orchestras. It was directed by Dr Kurt Singer, a neurologist, musicologist, conductor and, from 1927 to 1931, the Director of the German Opera House in Berlin. Singer emigrated to Holland in 1938 and from there he was deported to the concentration camp of Theresienstadt. He perished in Theresienstadt on 7 February 1944.

A special department of the Ministry of Propaganda headed by Hans Hinkel controlled the *Kulturbund.* He was a friend of Goebbels and most keen to please his friend and boss. In 1934, Hinkel prohibited the performance by Jews of plays by Friedrich Schiller, and in 1936 Johann Wolfgang von Goethe was also outlawed.

In 1937 Jewish orchestras were forbidden to play Beethoven, followed by Mozart in November 1938. The *Kulturbund* could play Händel, as he had blotted his copybook with the Nazis, because Händel had left Germany for England and he used too many themes from the Old Testament for his compositions. The activities of the *Kulturbund* became further restricted as the artists were drafted to do forced labour. On 11 September 1941, the Gestapo finally imprisoned the management of the *Kulturbund* and closed it down.

I remember experiencing many happy hours, together with family and friends, in the Freundesaal, which had been converted by the Breslau Jewish community into a theatre for the *Jüdischer Kulturbund.* When the *Kulturbund* was closed, there was something lacking in our lives. Although I should have had plenty of home studying to do, the lure of adventure, and the desire to get a break from the dreary and depressing routine of everyday life, was too great.

One day my three best friends, Hans Schwenk, Ulli Weissenberg and Klaus Stein, called, asking me to join them to go to a cinema. I did not say no. I should have known better. Some years back, a schoolmate got imprisoned for buying an ice-cream in a shop that had in its window a sign: *Juden unerwünscht* (Jews not wanted) and after just a few days in prison, his parents were asked to collect his ashes from the Gestapo office, as he had "died" in prison. My friends convinced me that it was safe to go to the cinema. The cinema we chose was near a quiet park wherein we could remove our "Yellow Star" and after the show reaffix it. We did not know which film was showing, but whatever it was, it was better than studying alone at home. We executed our plan with great precision, entering the cinema in the dark, and leaving it again before the lights came on.

The film was glorifying the triumphs of the German Army at this "heroic" stage of World War II. My ancestors had fought for Germany in the Napoleonic War, in the 1870-71 war and my father fought for four years in World War I. As a little boy, I used to play with his steel helmet and admire his Iron Cross. Was I to rejoice about the victories of the country that I once called my fatherland, or lament that these victorious battles would extend the suffering inflicted upon us, beyond the endurable? I did not enjoy a single moment of the film. I tried to find an answer to the question: What am I? German, Jew, or homeless and unwanted by any country into which we tried to emigrate? They all kept their doors and their hearts closed. Australia, my present home, stated in Parliament that it considered Hitler's persecution of the Jews a "European problem."

I had no desire for further outings, but the other three had acquired a taste for it, and the following day my friends called again. This time they suggested that we should go swimming in the Oder River. I declined to join them. In their eyes, I was a coward. My day passed with learning irregular Latin verbs. By evening, my parents arrived home from work, and soon after dark the mother of Hans called on us, sobbing, telling my parents that we boys had been to the pictures the day before and that today the other three had been swimming in the Oder River. Two of them claimed that they went home earlier than Hans. Hans had not yet arrived home. His mother was concerned that he would be out after the curfew for Jews. I could not help as I had not joined them and the other two would not say much.

The mystery was resolved very soon. The police reported that Hans's body had been found. He had drowned. The safe parts of the river set aside for swimming were for Aryans only. The lonely and dangerous part of the river where the boys had gone swimming had claimed its victim. The boys may have tried to help Hans when he got into trouble, but when they failed they may have been too frightened to call for help, and they hoped for a miracle. I never learnt the true facts of this matter. I often pondered, what would I have done if I had joined them?

Hans was an only son. His mother was a widow and now she was alone. We three remaining friends were not allowed to attend the funeral as we had done enough damage. I received a mighty hiding from my father and I had to spend the next day composing a letter of condolence to Hans' mother. My greatest punishment was that I had lost a good friend. I felt his loss deeply at the time and he has remained an integral part of my childhood memories. At the time, he was one of only four Jewish children left of the many hundreds with whom I had shared my early school years.

I managed to cope, not because I was unfeeling and callous, but by being constantly surrounded with death and decay, I must have felt intuitively then what I know now: "That death is inevitable, and it is only a question of how and when." The value of life is not the number of years lived, but the contribution made to the family of humankind during one's life. The day of Hans' funeral concluded the years of my childhood and thereafter the years of searching for the meaning of life had commenced.

The ghettoisation of the Jews of Breslau was completed in the second half of 1944. The last 200 to 300 Jews ended up in one street in Wallstrasse in *Judenhäusern* (houses for Jews only). Mr Herbert Marsch, an officer of the Breslau Gestapo, called on us in the Zimmerstrasse and inspected all the rooms of our five families. In the room of the family Jacob Cohen he discovered a beautiful Persian rug that was a reminder for them of better times. Marsch said to Jacob Cohen: "You have to vacate your dwelling within twenty-four hours; I like that Persian rug over there." Jacob Cohen replied: "Would you like to have it?" Marsch accepted the deal and replied: "You may stay an extra month in this place and the place you are going into will be quite comfortable." Cohen had the courage to ask Marsch to include us other families in the deal. Marsch kept his word. We could stay an extra month and got a reasonable three-room apartment for three families in the Wallstrasse 31. The Cohen family got the best room facing the street in consideration of their efforts. From this day on, we called them "die *Vorder-Cohens"*, because they had a room facing the street; the Max Kohns *"die Hinter-Kohns"*, because their room like ours faced a small dark back courtyard. Marsh cheated the other family out of the deal, and there was no comeback. We had to settle our part of the bargain with the "Front-Cohens" in bread, and that was harder currency than a Persian rug.

The forced labour at the chemical factory of Carl Böger & Co had drained all my remaining strength. The work entailed the unloading of rail trucks filled with 75kg bags of paint powder, the blending of different kinds of herbal teas to replace proper Chinese teas, which were in very short supply in Germany during the war, and the mixing of various fragrant essences with alcohol, and filling the resulting brew into perfume bottles. Depending on the daily work schedule, I came home some days with coloured underpants from the paint powder, on other days coughing from the lung irritation caused by the tea-dust, and sometimes smelling like a woman who does not know when to stop applying perfume. I was only a fifteen-year-old boy and it is surprising that carrying 75kg bags all day long, without sufficient food, did not cause any obvious long-term damage.

The railway siding where the unloading of the paint bags was done was a beehive of activity, and we worked side by side with French prisoners of war. They often had sympathy for me, and kindly put food they had stolen or received in POW food parcels into my coat pockets. The food was welcome, but it was also a threat to my life, because if the Gestapo had found it on me, the punishment for stealing food would have been meted out to me. It could have had most serious consequences.

In mid-1944 Jews were forbidden to assemble and consequently communal Jewish prayer had to cease in Breslau. This legislation was an incentive for some of us to defy it and to continue with our weekly Sabbath services in secret. About twenty of us met in the small bed-sitting-kitchen-room of the joiner Korotowski. We had to arrive at and leave his place in relays, to not arouse any suspicion. The traditional starting time of the Sabbath had to be ignored, due to a curfew that prevented us from being in the street after dark. Prayers were not sung but spoken in a whisper, to ensure that no sound could be heard in the stairwell. One of us was always on lookout roster and had to stand outside the entrance door of the apartment and knock whenever the sound of prayer could be heard outside Korotowski's little room. But these religious services gave us a great satisfaction, as they enabled us to maintain Jewish worship in this city where Jews had prayed for over a thousand years, until the last of us was deported.

Just before deportation, I contracted scarlet fever followed by heart complications. The large Jewish hospital in Breslau had long ago been transformed into a German military hospital and after a series of metamorphoses, the hospital for Jews had ended up in the small administration building of the Jewish cemetery. Everything was tried to cure me, but nothing seemed to fix the problem. My isolation room on the first floor of this makeshift hospital overlooked the many graves in this large cemetery. Somewhere out there was the family vault of my grandfather's brother's family and further away out of sight were the graves of my grandparents. The fact that Bärbel

Cohen, the daughter of the "Vorder-Cohens", had died just a few weeks earlier from the same disease, coupled with the view from my window over the graves, was not the best psychological support for an already difficult healing process. The last suggested treatment to hopefully save my life was a blood transfusion. Applications for blood was made by this makeshift Jewish hospital to the *Gesundheitsamt* (City Health Department). The reply was prompt: "The Nuremberg Laws for the protection of Aryan blood do not permit the use of Aryan blood by Jews." My father, although in no fit condition, gave of his blood. Shortly after this episode my father was deported into the labour camp of Gross Bargen.

My school friend Karla Wolff served as a general assistant in the hospital kitchen, and she also assisted with nursing and cleaning. She described in her booklet *Ich blieb Zurück* (I stayed behind), the life and events that went on around me, without me being aware of them, as I was tucked away in the infectious diseases room. The chief of the Jewish Department of the Breslau Gestapo, Walter Hampel, visited the hospital daily, and decided who could have an operation, who could stay a little longer, and who could work and had to be discharged. He never visited the first-floor rooms for infectious diseases where, apart from me, another patient suffering from tuberculosis was accommodated. His fear of infection was greater than his sense of duty.

The Gestapo had an observer in the operating theatre for every operation. Jewish women who became pregnant were destined to be deported for extermination before the birth of the child, so to prevent this from happening, the hospital conducted abortions to protect these women. The doctor had to invent some plausible explanation for these operations. The hospital probably would have been closed and its staff deported if the Gestapo observer had understood the true nature of this surgery. As soon as I got better, I was placed into the general ward of the hospital, and consequently I was soon found fit to resume my forced labour in the chemical factory.

In September 1944, it finally became my turn to begin the journey mapped out for all the Jews of Europe. I received a letter from the Gestapo to report on the following day to a rarely used and remote platform of the *Hauptbahnhof* (main railway station) of Breslau for deportation to a labour camp. As previously mentioned, my father had already preceded me. My mother had to stay behind to continue with her forced labour in a Breslau armaments factory. She prepared for me whatever suitable clothing I had left, and gave me all the available food in the house, leaving her with next to nothing. She was not allowed to see me off. Early in the morning we had to go on our separate ways.

Over the years, we had learnt to resist tears and drama, and thus avoid putting salt into open wounds. Her last words to me were: "Do not forget the key to our room." I assured her that I wouldn't forget it and that I would look after it. We both were aware that the key might never be used again, but to talk about it took the focus away from thinking about other less acceptable alternatives. Through the curtain I watched her walk along the street until she was out of sight, then I had a last look at our room, and left for my appointment at the station.

Just a few men of the remaining Jewish community were at the station. We were received by Herbert Marsch from the Gestapo office and locked into a compartment reserved for us on a train. Marsch travelled with us. He was remarkably polite and civilised, probably to avoid attracting any attention from the public. As the city of Breslau disappeared on the horizon, I knew that for the time being, I was on my own in this hostile world.

In conclusion let me state that I remember the Breslau Gestapo officers Marsch, Hampel and Wagner well, but I am not completely sure of their given names. Rumour has it that Marsch was beaten to death after the war, Hampel was arrested on 1 September 1948, but charges were not proceeded with in accordance with the British government's new war crimes policy; there does not appear to be any information available about the post-war fate of Wagner.

The Camps

> "The fish die when they are out of water, so do people die without law and order." *Talmud,* Abodah Zarah 4a

We arrived at a little village station called Gross Bargen after a couple of hours' journey and were ordered to leave the train. There Marsch handed us over to a camp guard who was already waiting for us. I tried to hang on to my luggage but it was taken from us and loaded onto a horse-drawn cart. We were given camp overalls. Under the supervision of the guard we had to load sugar beet onto some empty rail trucks at the station.

The guard shouted: "Move along otherwise you will arrive too late at the camp to get your food." It was late afternoon and I had not eaten anything since early morning. We worked as hard as we could so as not to miss out on the evening meal. The guard looked at me and shouted: "Where is your yellow star?" I had put on the camp overall and did not think that it would cover up my yellow star. I showed it to the guard under the overalls. He lectured me that it should be visible always. I was petrified, and pondered whether this was going to be the end of the story. It was a long cold day. We marched a few kilometres to our destination, the labour camp of Grünthal/Trachenberg. By the time we reached the camp in the evening, the guard had forgotten about my star. How lucky can you be?

The wooden barracks of the camp were empty and the entire camp appeared deserted. The inmates were all out working. I was shown to my bunk, given a paillasse that I had to fill with straw to serve as my mattress. I was also issued with wooden-soled working shoes, a thin overall and a shovel. Of course, the first job was to detach my yellow star from my coat and sew it onto my overalls in readiness for work the next day.

Where was the toilet? I followed the smell and found the latrine, an open pit with a wooden beam on its edge to sit upon. I soon learnt to be quick, to minimise the exposure to the stench arising from the contents of the pit. The lesson to be quick served me well, as at the onset of snowy weather and sub-zero temperatures, a quick job on the latrine became vital for survival.

On arrival, I could see the forest surrounding the camp which had been transformed by the setting sun into a fairyland of autumn colours. The willow trees lining the nearby Bartsch/ Barycz River completed the picture-postcard scenery.

I was brought back to the reality of the situation when a group of men with shovels over their shoulders, dressed in drab overalls and surrounded by camp guards, approached. They were singing marching songs. They looked thin and tired, and had to assemble first in front of the barracks for a roll call.

I realised that most were familiar faces, and among the men I discovered my father. We did not live in the same barrack. With little time to talk, we shared the leftover food my mother had given me in Breslau for this journey. It must have meant much more to father than just food. I had never seen my father cry, but he was doubtlessly greatly moved to see me again. At this moment, we both must have realised that the natural relationship between father and son had been brought to an abrupt end. He could no longer care for me, and I was unable to repay him with affection for his continuous love and guidance. Now, both of us were pawns in the deadly game Hitler had devised for his Jews. There were no words capable to express these feelings, nor was a cheap display of emotion appropriate at this moment. Out of the silence grew a deep affection of two kindred souls that was to stand the test of time for the rest of our lives.

It was getting dark and we had to queue up for a piece of rye bread and soup, in which floated bits of turnip and potato. There was a final rush to the latrine, because during the night curfew, it was the bucket inside the barrack. I was welcomed and bombarded with questions from my fellow barrack-dwellers about life in Breslau. Who was still left of the community?

The next day the repetitious work from dawn to dusk started for me. We had to dig deep anti-tank trenches in the loamy soil along the river Bartsch; fell pine trees in the nearby forest; carry them on our shoulders into the trenches, and stand on top of the willow trees at the river's edge and cut canes with an axe. In the winter months, it was an agonising job to stand on top of these trees in sub-zero temperatures, unable to move one's feet, and get the full blast of the wind blowing along the river valley. One side of the trench had a vertical wall held up by the trees rammed into the ground, on which were fastened the revetments made from the willow canes. The purpose of these trenches was to be an obstacle that would delay the advance of the Russian tanks into Germany.

My fellow inmates in the labour camp varied widely in age, educational, social and religious backgrounds. All of them were Jews in accordance with the definition of the Nuremberg Laws. Among them was a small group who, like us, wore the yellow star with the words *Jude* (Jew) on it, but who were Christians by religion. Some of them were baptised at birth and others had parents that had already been baptised.

While we quietly sang the Sabbath prayers and lit a few twigs in lieu of Chanukah candles, they would stick together and sing Christmas songs, which created a rather bizarre situation.

An elderly man who owned large textile mills before they were confiscated by the Nazis, was hounded to death, and the camp guards rejoiced when *der reiche Herr Kohn* (the rich Mr Kohn) was finally dead.

One day while felling trees in the forest, I discovered a dead young deer in the bushes. It had been shot, and probably the hunter could not find it. In temperatures well below zero, it was frozen hard. I brought it to the attention of Mr Nossen who came from a family of Jewish butchers. He suggested that we should take it to our barracks and there investigate its potential for food. At night, he carved it up and considered it to be a healthy animal. He cut out all the usable bits of meat, and then we had to decide how to cook it. We cleaned out one of the night ablution buckets with snow and sand, and boiled the meat in it on top of the small cast-iron stove in the centre of the barracks. It looked alright, smelled peculiar and was rather bland, but it was food that helped to give us a little extra strength. It was offered to everyone in our barracks, but there weren't many takers, which left a few of us with a good feed.

I remembered the Viennese Jewish writer Karl Kraus who pointed out in *Nachts* (1924) that everything acquired a subjective reality through the eyes of the observer: "The difference between an urn and a chamber-pot arises with the thought that one of these containers is being used for human remains, and the other for human waste." In fact, both are merely containers, and it is our subjective view of them that makes us consider one as being holy, and the other dirty. The deer meal out of the night bucket did not conform to any national cuisine and it also did not follow the kashrut requirements of Judaism. The deer meal was an object lesson to us that the human animal requires the necessary fuel for its body to survive, before our world-views can transform us into some higher form of life.

In this camp, my bedfellows were a rather mixed lot. A surgeon, an engineer specialising in the construction of water catchment retaining walls, an opera singer, a butcher and there was I, not even a schoolboy, as school had been prohibited for me. And yet, we had a lot in common. We all owned nothing, except our working clothes and a shovel. We shared the fact that our expert knowledge or the lack thereof and our status in life had become totally irrelevant. All that mattered was that we could dig anti-tank trenches all day long. But in one way we differed. Most of us supported one another, but there were a very few who were ready to steal the last piece of bread from their fellow inmates to increase their own chance of survival. In this way camp life highlighted the difference between those who had remained a human being, and those who had deteriorated into merely being a human animal. This experience has remained deeply ingrained in my psyche to this very day. Whenever I meet people, I ask myself the question: "If all they own, know and stand for would be taken away from them, would they then be reduced to a human being or a human animal?" The Holocaust teaches that we need to develop this elusive quality which determines good or evil in our actions and thereby gives hope to future generations.

As winter progressed, the rumbling noise of artillery fire could be heard in the distance. As it came closer, instead of being led to work and continue digging tank-trap-trenches, all the inmates of the labour camp in Grünthal had to pack their few belongings and stand to attention on the rollcall ground. It was a cold and frosty day. The whole camp was going to be moved. To where? No one knew.

A Jewish lawyer from the city of Görlitz, who had served in the German Army in World War I, kept on telling us that we should march in a more exacting military fashion to earn the respect of the camp commander. He meant well, but was shouted down and asked to mind his own business and not try to outdo the Gestapo. Suddenly he keeled over right next to me, and died instantly. He had no family with him. His openly expressed thoughts that part of the cause of the persecution of the Jews was self-inflicted by being nonconformists and insufficiently attuned to German national pride, had isolated him from the majority. I felt no one was upset by his death. Life was cheap. Too many had died to make one identify with every individual tragedy. I cannot help but remember him with sorrow, because he was a symbol of desperate loneliness among a mass of people. Every human being dies for him or herself alone, while the rest of the family of man keeps on walking along the path of history. Hans Fallada's 1947 novel *Jeder stirbt für sich allein (Every Man Dies Alone)* was one of the first anti-Nazi novels to be published by a German author after World War II. The novel expresses the feeling of loneliness that comes with trying to walk along the right path within a crowd that acts like a flock of sheep.

The camp commander assigned the butcher Nossen and me to bury the body in a ditch on the side of the road. There was no point to it, as the soil was frozen hard. We covered him with his coat and some pine tree branches, trusting that the falling snow would do the rest.

German peasants were abandoning their farms and going on the "track" into central Germany. Nossen said to me that he was going to flee and hide in an empty farmhouse, waiting for the Russian Army to overtake him. He asked me to join him. I was not yet ready to play such high stakes and risk my life. I rejoined the camp inmates.

It was an eerie scene. German soldiers were marching in the opposite direction to us, towards the Russian front. Peasants with horse and cart and their belongings were moving towards Central Germany. We were marching into Germany to a yet unknown destination. Before us marched Hungarian Jews from Auschwitz on the way to Dachau and Bergen-Belsen. Now and then we had to stop and remove the bodies of Jewish women in concentration camp clothing, who had collapsed on the road. At night, we slept in abandoned farmhouses on the floor, close together to keep warm. As we moved past abandoned manors, the cries of pain of cows left behind in the stables and not milked for days aroused our pity for these suffering animals.

After some days of wandering with little food and sore feet from our wooden shoes, we arrived at a new camp, the concentration camp of Gross-Rosen. Our labour camp commander arranged a guard for us as he entered the camp to hand us over. We waited for hours in the cold and snow. A young SS guard came up to me, lit a cigarette and offered me one out of his packet. I did not smoke. I did not know what to do. What was the catch? He shouted that I should take it. I took it and smoked my first cigarette. I looked at him from the corner of my eye. Had his world that had collapsed around him helped him to discover some feeling of sympathy for a fellow human being, or did he merely think this public gesture would make all of us feel at ease, and make us believe that we were about to settle down in a friendly place?

Our camp commander appeared very agitated. The inmates of Gross-Rosen were preparing to move into Central

Germany soon, and was not ready to receive us just yet. We had to sleep the night in a nearby dance hall of the Gross-Rosen village inn. No food was issued. Night fell, and one of our fellow prisoners played Mozart on the dance-hall grand piano. I had a foul taste in my mouth from the cigarette.

It was soon silent, as everybody fell asleep from sheer exhaustion.

Christmas Trees

> "To the Jews only, and not to the Gentiles, was a Saviour promised." – Elias Hicks (1748-1830)

The concentration camp of Gross-Rosen was situated about 60 kilometres southwest of Breslau. It was established in 1939 as a sub-camp of the concentration camp of Sachsenhausen to accommodate Polish prisoners of war. These prisoners had to work as forced labourers in the nearby granite quarries. Jews were not sent to this camp until 1943. After 1943 the camp's population increased rapidly and therefore several satellite camps had to be established. SS Sturmbannführer Johannes Hassebroek was the commander of the camp from October 1943 until its evacuation on 14 February 1945. He was sentenced to death by the British after the war for atrocities committed by him, but the death sentence was not carried out and he was released after a relatively short prison term. In an interview with the

Israeli historian Tom Segev he said: "All I know about the atrocities at Gross-Rosen I learnt during the trials against me."

A conflict within the Nazi leadership was the cause of the growth of Gross-Rosen. Some wanted to exterminate Jews as quickly as possible, while others wanted to work them first to exhaustion and death in the German war industry. By 1943 the German Luftwaffe had become less effective and to keep the German war industry out of the reach of the allied bomber command, more and more arms production was relocated to the East.

Entrance to the concentration camp of Gross-Rosen. Muzeum Gross-Rosen w Rogoznizy

When I arrived in Gross-Rosen, the Third Reich was already in a state of collapse and the treatment of prisoners in this camp was no longer following the directives of the Gestapo in Berlin, but was subject to the ad hoc decisions of the camp commander. Some of his decisions went even beyond the inhuman guidelines of the Gestapo headquarters. A book written by Bella Gutterman and published by Yad Vashem *(Narrow Bridge to Life, the Gross-Rosen Network of Labour Camps for Jews),* reports in detail about the great hardships experienced in Gross-Rosen during the final months of the war. In October 1944, seven children were born to women in the camp and on orders of the camp commander they were killed as soon as they emerged from the mother's womb. Food and supplies were planned to be just below subsistence level, but in addition the SS guards sold the little food available for prisoners on the black market to enrich themselves. Thousands of prisoners from concentration camps east of Gross-Rosen flowed into the camp daily and its population was starting to exceed 40,000. Some of the SS guards were drafted to join the German fighting forces and they were replaced with Hitler Youth and *Volkssturm* (Home Guards).

Conditions in the camp became chaotic. By early 1945, the Russian Army had liberated Poland, reached the Oder River, and started to occupy Silesia. All inmates of Gross-Rosen were planned to be moved into the concentration camps in the still unoccupied Germany. The Red Army had already reached Küstrin and was racing towards Berlin, thus threatening to cut off Silesia from Central Germany. So for the Nazis to complete the evacuation of Gross-Rosen by February 1945 was a matter of urgency.

Once again, we could hear the rumbling noise of the Russian artillery in the distance. In January 1945, we were still in reasonable shape compared to the longer-term prisoners of the camp, so our ex-Grünthal group was among the first to be sent on the march into central German concentration camps. Fortunately, my stay in Gross-Rosen was brief enough to give me a better chance of survival. We passed through Jauer, the nearest small town to the camp, with a population of 13,700 inhabitants. The winter of 1945 was very cold in Germany, and at times temperatures dropped to below minus 20 degrees centigrade. I had seen the result of the death marches on my way to Gross-Rosen, and was now faced with the choice to either continue marching with the group along the road to the next concentration camp and possibly become one of those many frozen bodies to be placed into the ditch by the side of the road, or risk an escape. The second option, if caught, would result in being shot or hanged instantly without trial.

Seeing a few overcrowded trains in the town's small railway station helped me to make the decision to escape and try to live underground. Being still in civilian clothing of sorts, I boarded one of these trains. Train tickets were no longer required, a fact I was not aware of until I reached the railway station. I did not own any money, and this fact alone shows that I was an amateur fugitive who was totally unprepared for the escape. I spent most of the time hiding in the train's lavatory and I was sorely aware that from now on, being discovered would mean instant execution by the Gestapo.

I realised that I needed help to survive. The odds were stacked against me, and hoping that luck would continue to be on my side was unrealistic. The train took me 280 kilometres into Germany, and I succeeded in making my way to the city of Halberstadt where we had relatives living in a privileged mixed marriage. I did not know them very well at that time, but they received me most cordially and they were overjoyed to find me still alive. However, it did not take long for them and for me to fully comprehend that my presence in their midst endangered their lives and that I could not expect to be sheltered in their home for any length of time.

Had I arranged for my own death sentence by escaping, without securing a permanent hiding place for myself? The problem was solved during the following night. The air-raid sirens went off late in the evening, and everyone went down into the air-raid shelter. Suddenly I realised that I could not join the others in the shelter, as everybody knew everyone else and the question would be raised: "Who was I?"

At that time, the beautiful mediaeval town of Halberstadt was still untouched by bombing raids. I stood at the open window overlooking the city. Suddenly four beautiful flares looking like Christmas trees came sailing down slowly from the sky, defining the square within where the city was located. There was the droning of aeroplane engines, and then all hell broke loose. As the planes travelled over this square, they dropped their loads of explosives and incendiary bombs. All around me the old town sank into ruins.

From this raid, Halberstadt was 82 per cent destroyed and 8000 people died, as I watched these most spectacular fireworks. The room in which I was meant to sleep that night had a hole in the ceiling. A bomb had entered the room, torn the bed apart, disappeared through the floor and had come to rest on the floor below without exploding. The terror came to an end within the hour and only the shouting of the rescue teams, the crying of the wounded, the lament of those who had lost loved ones and all their belongings, and the roar of the fire, could be heard.

It was well past midnight. I had only a few hours left to decide on the next move for survival. There were few options that remained. I had no connections to an underground movement, I was a total stranger in Halberstadt and I had none of the papers required to identify myself to the satisfaction of the authorities in the tightly controlled German society. The goodbye from my family was without drama, but they must have been aware that my chances of survivinge after leaving their home were only very slim. We all realised that I could not stay with them without endangering all our lives. I had no right to inflict my fate upon them.

We parted with mixed feelings of affection, fear and disappointment, and on my part, gratitude for the few hours of respite from my life of a fugitive. It was early morning, and I wandered aimlessly through the streets of

Halberstadt, past piles of dead bodies. I realised that I had to try and move on so I headed towards the railway station. Little was left of the station. I was grateful to be alive and to have survived up to this point.

I did not hold God responsible for the terror of the years from 1933 to 1945 and nor did I credit God for having spared me during this bombing. The recognition of the greatness of this universe, and the kindness residing within so many human beings, had survived within me, unimpaired through this night of terror that killed and spared the guilty and the innocent alike.

The last rabbi of German Jewry, Dr Leo Baeck, once wrote: "Christianity is the religion believing in exterior salvation; Judaism is the religion requiring interior redemption." I felt grateful that the accident of my birth allowed me to grow up in the latter tradition. After it is all over, a lot of work will have to be done by humanity to redeem itself through its own efforts. To believe in being saved – as the Apostle Paul put it: *sola fide* (by faith alone) – is hiding oneself from reality and responsibility, and running after a pipe dream.

Loam and Vinegar

> *"Optimum est pati quod emendare non possis."* (It is best to endure what you cannot change.)
> – Lucius Anneaus Seneca (4 BCE–65 CE)

The Halberstadt railway station had been destroyed and there was now a ditch where once there used to be a rail track. An ammunition transport train had been standing on that track when it received a full hit in the air raid.

Despite the early hour of the morning the station was crowded with people. Suddenly, a lady came running up to me and greeted me: "Good day, Mr Schmidt. Good to see you. You will find many friends from Breslau here." She disappeared into the crowd without waiting for a response. I was petrified with shock and fear. She was once a neighbour of ours in Breslau and knew me well. Had she rushed away to report me to the authorities? Why did she call me Mr Schmidt, when she knew only too well that my name was Aufrichtig? Why did she tell me about the many friends from Breslau? Twelve years of Nazi rule were unable to shatter my belief in the goodness that resides in most people. I interpreted her strange action as a desire to warn me to be careful not to be recognised and that I needed to change my identity. She probably left so hurriedly because she was frightened to talk to a Jewish fugitive. I was shaken to the core through this unexpected encounter, and it sensitised me to suitably adjust my behaviour and take extra care in my new life ahead.

Halberstadt Railway Station nowadays.

At the end of the railway platform was a small waiting room. In it sat an official who issued temporary *Kennkarten* (Identification cards) and a small amount of money. He also allocated the people who had lost everything in the air raid to trains that were waiting on the repaired track ready to take them to a place of work and shelter in a more remote part of Germany. I joined the long queue and gave the official a false name and address. It worked! But when I think back, I must have been crazy to have used my mother's maiden name, kept my correct given name, changed my birth date just by one month only and used my correct place of birth. The form also asked for religion which I stated as *Evangelisch* (Protestant). The false details were too close for comfort to properly conceal my real identity, but then I was not used to adopting aliases every day, and there was little time available for me to scheme and think more clearly.

My father went through the same procedure independently. We kept our distance from one another in order not to endanger each other's life should we be found out.

After a 200-kilometre journey south, the train arrived in Tirschenreuth, a small picturesque town (9100 inhabitants) in the Fichtelgebirge. I spent most of the journey with my cap drawn over my face pretending to be asleep, or stayed if possible in the toilet of the train out of fear of being recognised. The train had an anti-aircraft-gun carriage, making me aware of new dangers facing my life. However, these risks I shared with the rest of the German population. On arrival, we had to assemble in the dancehall of a small inn, and from there we were allocated to farms in which to work and to live. A bus took me to the small village of Neudorf in Oberfranken close to the Czech border.

The bus driver dropped me at the gate of a farm belonging to the Häckl family. The farm was built as an enclosed square. In the front was a great wooden gate, flanked on the left by a workshop and on the right by the living quarters of the farmer's son. Above the gate was the *Stadl* (hayloft). Further back the buildings on the right were stables for the cattle, and the building on the left-hand side were the farmer's living quarters. The square was closed at the back with a building housing the farm machinery, and on top of it was the threshing floor to separate the chaff and straw from the grain. Around the entire complex was a continuous iron rail so that the watchdog could move around the building and protect the circumference of the farmyard. In the centre court was an enormous heap of manure that rested on iron grates, under which was a basin catching the rainwater that flowed through the animal manure, transforming it into liquid fertiliser. In front of it all was a pond for the farming of carp.

The farmer and his wife must have been in their sixties, and the whole family, including me, addressed them as father and mother Häckl. I cannot remember their first names, or more precisely, I never got to know what they were. Their younger unmarried son Alois lived with them. He had been wounded in the war and walked with difficulty. Their unmarried daughter Lena also lived and worked on the farm. She had a slightly dislocated hip from birth, and therefore also had walking problems. Their oldest son was represented in every room by photos flanked with vases full of fresh flowers. He had been killed in action in the war, and was the son the family had given to the Catholic Church as a priest. He had served in a church in the nearby village of Konnersreuth, where the mystic Therese Neumann displayed the stigmata every year at Easter.

I was a very welcome farm worker. I received a room in the attic above the stables and meals at the family table in lieu of payment. It was for me a time for learning. How to plough the fields with oxen, to fell trees, to milk cows, and to do all kinds of work, and enjoy the satisfaction that comes from working with one's hands. Most of all, it was an opportunity to discover that, during the turmoil of war, these hard-working, decent and kindly people, with their child-like and simple faith, were to me like an oasis in the desert.

I knew very little about Christianity, so to consolidate my alibi, at night I read the New Testament for the first time. It was most difficult for me to understand how a nation could worship a non-Aryan as a part of their God, could read from a book that contains so much of the wisdom of Israel and call their faith the "religion of love", while practising so much hate and condemning Judaism as the "religion of law". Did it never occur to them that they too were suffering from the curse of a lawless society they had created for themselves?

Germany for the Häckls was the soil of the fields they and their forebears had tilled for generations, the small corner of forest from which they cut the timber to build their farm and collected their firewood. German was their mother tongue, the only language they knew and spoke with a broad Franconian accent.

Christianity was for them to live a simple, decent life and to pray before and after every meal the way they had learnt to pray from their parents and from their priest in the parish church. Every Sunday they would walk four kilometres to Konnersreuth and home again after having partaken in the

Eucharist at their beloved church. They closed the farm and asked me to join them. It was fortunate that I had stated Protestant as religion in my false papers and therefore could graciously decline their offer. In response, they directed me to the location of the nearest Protestant church and I had to leave the farm at the same time as they did. I obviously did not go to church, but walked through the winter forest until sufficient time had elapsed to allow me to return to their home. They never asked any questions about my Sunday morning outing. Maybe the Catholic religion was to them the only reality in their lives and other religions were beyond their ken.

On 26 July 1943, in a tirade of hate at his headquarters, Hitler, who also was a Catholic, said to General Karl Friedrich Otto Wolff: "I would go straight into the Vatican. Do you think the Vatican impresses me? I could not care less ... We will clear out that gang of swine ... Then we will apologise for it afterwards ... I could not care less." On 9 September 1943, Wolff, who was by then supreme commander of the SS and German police in Italy, was flown to Hitler's headquarters in East Prussia to discuss the "Occupation of the Vatican by the SS and the transfer of Pope Pius XII to Liechtenstein."

I feel sure the Häckls did not know, and did not want to know about Hitler's crimes and his future sinister plans. Their hard work, love for their land, and their unfaltering faith, was sheltering their lives from the turmoil that plagued the world beyond the beautiful mountains and forest of the Fichtelgebirge.

On my Sunday walks, with my father, I used to have the opportunity to think about my own Jewish tradition, about family and friends who had been taken away, and about the future, should I live to see it. How would I be able to rebuild the foundation for a new life on the quicksand of my unique experiences of the past? *"Adonai Hu Ha-elohim"* (The Eternal is our God) is the final prayer a Jew should utter before dying. I often remembered these three words of wisdom. They make one recognise the greatness of time and space vis-à-vis the smallness of our human existence. They encourage gratitude for the opportunities this life has to offer and the commitment to live every moment to the fullest.

The shared Sunday meal after returning home was always a sobering experience. We all sat around the big wooden table and a large bowl of hot nourishing food was placed in the middle. A home baked ryebread was passed around, and everyone cut off a big piece. There were no individual plates but we all ate with our own spoons out of the same dish. The meal was usually a mixture of meat, potatoes and vegetables. What type of meat? I did not ask any questions. There is a principle in Judaism called *"P'kuach Nefesh"* (to preserve a soul). All ritual laws are overridden to preserve a life. In any case, I had grown up in a liberal Jewish home which placed greater emphasis on what comes out of the mouth rather on that which goes into the mouth. After the meal, we had to milk the cows, feed the animals, and clean up the stables. Every animal had a name and, before approaching it from the behind, you had to call out its name and talk to it, enabling you to move it to replace the straw underneath without being kicked by the animal.

Life rolled along without a hitch, until one day I developed an infection in a joint of the index finger of my left hand which refused to heal. It needed medical attention, but what was the use of my finger if the rest of me was exposed to undue risk? Would I need an anaesthetic? At that time my perception was that while counting oneself to sleep as the nurse dripped *ether pro narcosi* on the face mask, some patients talked in their state of confusion. Might I be one of those patients who would talk under the influence of the ether-anaesthetic and reveal my identity?

I had to try and fix my finger without consulting a doctor. The farmer's family proudly offered some well-tried home remedies that they assured me would work. First day, leaves of a tree tied on the finger; second day, chewed rye bread and the final attempt was to cover the finger with loam and pour vinegar on the loam. However, nothing stopped the infection's progress and I had to bow to the inevitable and walk six kilometres to the Waldsassen hospital for the lancing of the finger, a treatment done under anaesthetic. It went well, but the hospital could not keep me as an in-patient as it had to attend to a constant stream of wounded German soldiers.

After resting for a few hours, I walked the six kilometres back home. Allied fighter aircraft no longer had to deal with the German Luftwaffe, so to keep busy, they directed their machine guns at farmers and cattle in the fields. Consequently, my long walk home after the operation was interrupted now and again by having to seek shelter in a ditch on the side of the road near a tree to escape the hail of bullets. This reassured me that no one has a monopoly on acts of inhumanity.

Winter changed into spring and as Easter approached the peasants placed a twig of pussy willow, which had been blessed by the Church, into the corner of every field. This was done to ensure that they would have a good harvest. Passing these symbols of spring and regrowth reminded me that the time for Passover must come soon. I did not have a Jewish calendar and I could not take notice of Passover in this, my alternative life. This Festival of Freedom would have to wait for me until freedom had been granted to me again.

Each year at Passover, as we read the story of the beginning of the journey of the Jewish people through history, I recall my part of that journey, the wonderful places I have seen, and the great people I have met along the way. I hope that my children and their children will learn from the wisdom gained from the Jewish experience, that life is not a safe house in which to live, but an exciting and sometimes dangerous journey along a never-ending road. The reward for making the journey is the encounter with people and the opportunity to experience our colourful world along this road. The yearning for ever-new adventures instils within us the will to live, and teaches us the art of survival.

Schwanzparade

"Defeat serves to enlighten us."
– Johann Kasper Lavater (1741-1801)

Just a few days before my sixteenth birthday, on 16 April 1945, I received a registered letter at the Häckle's farm, ordering me to report to Tirschenreuth, the nearest administrative town, for an army medical examination. I was summoned to join Hitler's Wehrmacht and to defend the Third Reich, if found medically fit. The end of the war was in sight and I had survived so far. I had only two options. Not to attend, and risk being strung up on the next tree for refusing to follow the call of duty to the Führer, or to attend the medical examination and risk revealing my true Jewish identity, and possibly be executed as a concentration camp escapee. In the forests of the Fichtelgebirge, the final battles for the remaining German sovereign territory were taking place, and to try and hide there was not likely to succeed.

I had no real choice. A final decision had been made for me. All that was left was the hope that there would still be a life after the dreaded call-up-date. Who knows, the war might end before then! But my luck had run out. In Upper Franconia, the war did not end before 16 April 1945.

It was a warm sunny spring morning and the tender young growth in the fields and forests transformed the countryside into a fairyland of colour and great beauty. It felt like starting out on a holiday, but it was a journey to an appointment that would determine my future – was it to be life or death? The road to Tirschenreuth was crowded with the last vehicles of the German Army, retreating from Czechoslovakia. Many times, soldiers offered me a lift on their army trucks. I refused. The scent of spring, the warm sun and the awakening of nature sustained me on the sixteen kilometres of my journey.

I arrived at the City Council building of Tirschenreuth, filled in the required form using my false identity, stripped naked and stood with many other German boys of the same age before the army doctor and army officers. The German nickname for this procedure is *Schwanzparade* (parade of the tails). The moment of truth had arrived. My tail looked different to that of all the other boys. I did not enjoy the luxury, to have Jesus circumcised on my behalf, an event which some churches still celebrate on 1 January every year, eight days after his assumed birth on 25 December.

The doctor listened to my chest, looked in my mouth, and asked me which type of military unit I would prefer. I had thought ahead and without hesitation replied, the "Parachute Regiment". The German Air Force was in a total state of disarray and therefore I was hoping this would delay matters. He commended me for my expression of bravery, but he said the more immediate need of the Fatherland was for infantry units and, being the tallest of the group and a very Aryan type, he would recommend me to the Waffen SS. We had to get dressed, go home and would be advised shortly where to report for military service.

To step back into the fresh air and the sunlight and still be alive was one of the greatest moments of my life, true joie-de-vivre. What had happened? Was it that, after six million Jews had been abandoned, God had remembered that I had kept my part of the covenant by circumcision and it was time for God to honour His part of the covenant? Or was it merely the incompetence of the army doctor not to see the anatomical difference between me and the other boys? Was it the doctor's desire to avoid messy problems at this late stage of his military career? Or did the doctor have a diabolical sense of humour and it tickled his fancy to promote an Aryan-looking Jew to be Hitler's instrument for bringing about the "final solution" to the Jewish problem?

More urgent thoughts came to the fore. My problem of life and death had not been solved, but had merely been postponed. As I walked the sixteen kilometres back home, the stream of the retreating German soldiers still flowed along the road. This time, as I now walked in the opposite direction, I could see the despondent battle-weary faces. The gruesome reality of the situation became more and more clear to me. Was I going to put on the battle-dress of the executioners when called up for military service? Would it not be better to share the fate of my fellow Jews to be shot as a Jew, rather than be shot for the crimes I had to suffer for, but did not commit? Should I report to the army, take the rifle and sit out these last days of the war in the forest? Was this realistic? I had never fired a rifle before in my life. Or should I accept the rifle, and fire the first bullet through my head at a time and place of my choosing, rather than give others the satisfaction of having eliminated yet another Jew? I tried to find an answer to these questions on the long way home. Was it possible to find a balance between survival, sanity and integrity?

I arrived back at the farm and the farmer and his family wanted to know what had happened. It was spring and time for the clover to be cut in the fields, seed-potatoes to be put into the ground, and some fields needed to be ploughed and seeded. Would I still be available to share in this work, or would I have to leave the farm for the army? I suspected there was more than that on their mind. The old couple were not only concerned about losing a much-needed worker, but they had come to appreciate my contribution to their land, their herd of animals and their farm, which had been in their family's care for generations. Although it was only a few months since our lives had been thrown together by fate, affection and mutual respect had become a bond between us.

The old couple had lost a son in the battle of Stalingrad and the possibility of me sharing their son's fate in these last days of the war, must have, no doubt, crossed their minds. I put on my work clothes and joined them in the work we had already been doing together for several days: sorting out a large heap of potatoes into those best suited for seeding and the remainder to be used as fodder for the animals. Little was said, but from time to time our eyes met, revealing our unspoken thoughts.

Day after day passed, filled with hard work from dawn to dusk, and with the yearning to survive this terrible Holocaust.

The war ended with Germany's unconditional surrender, on 7 May 1945 – before the army called me up. I often wonder what I would have done if forced to choose between my survival and my religion. I promised myself never to judge a fellow human being before I have better understood my own self. I am still searching for this understanding. But for the last month of the war, hard work and the hope for survival filled every hour of the day.

Loewenstein

"Freedom is a new religion, the religion of our time." – Heinrich Heine (1797-1856)

The Häckls did not get a newspaper and they were not in the habit of listening to the wireless. The German news broadcasts were propagandist, and they did not give accurate information at the best of times. Alois listened secretly to the BBC at night. He must have been reasonably well informed about the political situation, but he was too frightened to share this knowledge with the rest of us. At that time, I did not know that the American Army had occupied Nuremberg on 20 April 1945, which was situated a mere 90 kilometres west from us, and that the Soviet troops had already entered Berlin. This knowledge would have greatly relieved my anxiety while waiting to be called up by the German Army.

On the evening of 30 April, the farmer living opposite our farmhouse came bursting into the room telling us that Adolf Hitler had committed suicide.

He was greatly distressed, for good reason. He was the local *Ortsgruppenleiter* (representative of the Nazi Party) who was still talking about an *Endsieg* (final victory), and who gave the order that nobody in the village should surrender. On 7 and 9 May 1945, Germany unconditionally surrendered in Rheims and Berlin, but the political situation in the village of Neudorf remained uncertain.

The flow of vehicles of the retreating German Army had come to an end. A lone German Army vehicle stopped in front of the Nazi Party representative's farmhouse opposite the Haeckels' farm. Several Waffen-SS soldiers entered his house to advise him that the German Army was retreating and that American troops were likely to enter the village shortly. After these soldiers left, all was quiet and peaceful in the village and there was only occasional rifle and machine gun fire to be heard in the nearby forest. The American military reconnaissance was right on the ball. The German Army vehicle had just left the Nazi's farm, when a direct hit of an artillery shell set that farmhouse alight.

Above their stable was the hayloft filled with straw and hay. The old farmhouse burned with a roar, and the fire rose towards heaven like a torch. There was no loss of human life, but the intense heat burned chickens alive in the enclosed farmyard and screaming cattle burned to death in the stable. The Nazi farmer informed the village about the forthcoming likely events, and asked everybody to do their duty, without being able to define what duty could be performed.

This one and only artillery shell that exploded in Neudorf had an effect as though a lid had been taken off a pressure-cooker. The peasants were no longer afraid of Nazi rule and they hung big white bed-sheets out of the windows of their farmhouses as a sign of surrender. Only a few days earlier, such action would have cost them their lives. Normal life stopped in the village and all sat silently together in the cellars of their farmhouses. I quietly sneaked out and stood in front of the farmhouse in bright sunshine overlooking the rolling fields surrounding it. The "Amis" were coming across these fields, spread out widely with their weapons ready for action. I must have taken leave of my senses.

Why should they not shoot at a "German" standing in their way?

As the troops came closer, one of the soldiers came towards me. "Are there still German soldiers in the village?" he asked in perfect German.

"There are none, to the best of my knowledge. You can trust me, I am a Jew living in hiding," I replied.

"I was also a German Jew. My family migrated to the USA and I live in New York. My name is Loewenstein. There are still pockets of SS about. Wait before you reveal to anyone who you are, until a military administration had been firmly established," he replied.

We never met again. But these few shared moments remain a unique experience for me, raising again and again the question: What are we? Germans, Americans, Australians or Jews? I think we are all that, and more. We are members of the family of humanity, regardless whether we are wanted or not by our fellow human beings. We all share in all the joys and suffering of this world.

There we stood facing each other, descendants of Jewish families who had lived in Germany for generations, who had suffered recent persecution and who once had found shelter within its borders for centuries. Our ancestors had entered Germany as slaves with the Roman Army and our families, over two thousand years of history, had advanced to be proud "German citizens of the Jewish faith" until the advent of Hitler's rule of terror.

The American soldier Loewenstein had to fight on and occupy the next village. I had to go back and continue preparing potatoes for seeding and to place them into the awakening soil. As I continued to sort the seed potatoes, my mind kept on wandering, and I suddenly remembered a rabbinic commentary on the creation legend: "The question was raised: why does all humanity descend from one man, Adam?" The answer was given: "So that none of us can ever say that my ancestors are better than yours." Somewhere along the course of history, we Jews have failed to properly tell this parable to the world.

Whenever I see film clips how the end of World War II was celebrated around the world with rejoicing and exuberance, I am most grateful for having been denied this opportunity. It has taken me a lifetime to comprehend the loss of 55 million lives between 1939 and 1935, the loss and destruction of so much that was beautiful and good and the brutalisation of so many human minds from which the world has not yet recovered completely.

I did not stay in Neudorf for long enough to see the seed potatoes I sorted on the last day of the war bear fruit and sustain the hungry. I do not think I shall stay in this world for long enough to see the seeds for human understanding planted by those who lived through the Holocaust ripen into fruition.

Holy Water

"The soul that sees beauty may sometimes walk alone." – Johann Wolfgang von Goethe (1749-1832)

Spring brought with it the requirement for a lot of hard work. Clover had to be cut to provide the first green feed for the farm animals, the cows were calving, potatoes and fodder beets were planted and the liquid animal manure had to be pumped out of the basin from underneath the big dung heap. The farm had neither horses nor tractors, so I drove for many hours with an ox-cart over the fields. A large tank filled with the liquid manure was mounted on this cart, to spread the precious liquid over the crops.

I became drenched in liquid manure from the over-spray and I had to soak in the bath every night. The bathtub had to be carried into the kitchen from the machinery shed and there it was filled with hot water. The kitchen wood stove was surrounded with a large water tank, and the hot water was laboriously transferred from it into the bathtub with a jug. Quite often I needed to pick scraps of food off my body that had fallen from the cooking pots into the tank. The longer daylight hours provided more time to work in the fields and the hours for sleeping were reduced.

In the privacy of my sleeping quarters, I recovered from the inside lining of my jacket the "Yellow Star of David" and my "Jewish Identity Card". This card was over-printed with a big "J" for Jew, and the obligatory first name "Israel" was added to my given name. Every day I wondered when and where an American military administration would be established in the district.

At long last, on 28 May 1945, I was able to walk again the sixteen kilometres to Tirschenreuth and present myself, equipped with my precious documents, to the Americans. After due investigation, I received an up-to-date identity card reaffirming my proper personal details, and a letter from the US Army requesting that, as a victim of fascism, I should be given every assistance to enable me to return to my hometown of Breslau. I did not know that merely three months earlier, on 4 February 1945, the four Allied powers had decided at the Conference of Yalta to give the German province of Silesia and its capital city Breslau to Poland. I could not anticipate that my journey to Breslau to find my family would require me to cross illegally from the American Zone into the Russian Zone of Germany and thereafter to again illegally travel from the Russian Zone into that previously German territory which had now become part of Poland.

May was a very busy time on the farm, and the farmer depended on my labour. How was I going to tell the family who had saved my life that I wanted to leave them, at a time when they most needed my help? How would they react when they were going to learn that, unbeknown to them, they had given shelter to a Jew? In their simple faith, they truly believed in the infallibility of the Pope and that their beloved Catholic Church was the only Church in possession of the truth. They did not know that thousands of Jews had been murdered and that their Church had destroyed hundreds of Jewish communities during the Crusades and the Spanish Inquisition. They had not been taught that Jews were tortured to death, falsely accused of desecrating the Host, of blood libel, of poisoning wells, of causing the plague, of killing Christ and of preaching falsehoods. At that time on Good Friday, the words *pro perfidis Judaeis* (perfidious Jews) were still part of the Catholic liturgy, but they were said in Latin and consequently the malicious meaning of these words was lost on them.

It was a mild spring evening, the perfume of the flowering plants filled the air, and the last rays of the setting sun gilded the entire land. We were sitting together, recovering after a heavy day's work, when I broke the silence and told them my story in very simple words. It took a while for them to realise that it was not just a story, but the history of my life. Their eyes were moist and I too found it hard to stay detached. We experienced that all our differences had now become insignificant and that we had developed a deep affection for one another. There was a long silence. Then the old woman spoke: "We still do love you. After all, Jews are human beings too," and she grabbed me for a most cordial embrace that said it all.

It was a blow to them that I wanted to leave immediately and return to the city of my birth, to find out who of the family had survived. All I owned fitted into one rucksack and took no time to pack. The following morning, I was ready to leave the farm on foot, well equipped with food and drink to last for a few days. Mother Häckl had risen early and left to get me a farewell gift. She had walked six kilometres to the next village to visit her parish church in Konnersreuth. There she got for me a large bottle of holy water to take along with me, so that my homeward journey would be safe and blessed. It was indeed holy water, not because it was blessed by the Church, but because it came from the wells of goodness that were within these simple farmers and that are potentially within every human being.

As I walked away across the fields into the distant forest, the whole family was waving farewell for a long time. The weather became warmer and the large bottle of holy water was an awkward part of my luggage. What should I do with it? I remembered the lesson of the Prophet Jeremiah who taught: "You shall pray for the country in which you reside." We had lived in Germany for so long, and at the low point of its history I found it appropriate to gently empty the holy water upon its soil and to hope and pray that the deep wounds, suffered by all within its borders would soon heal. After walking and hitchhiking for some 300 kilometres, I arrived in Halberstadt, the place where I had first found shelter after escaping from the concentration camp of Gross-Rosen.

I suddenly became desperately ill and a doctor had to be my first port of call. He diagnosed my illness to be typhoid. Typhoid was very common in Germany as the bombing caused drinking water to be contaminated with waste from sewerage pipes, making water a dangerous substance unless it was well boiled to kill bacteria.

The letter from the US Army in Tirschenreuth requesting that I be given help to return home after my Holocaust experience allowed me to be admitted for medical care into an American Army hospital. I was lucky to be placed there, as a normal German hospital, at that time, would not have had access to sophisticated antibiotics.

I was delirious for several days and in a coma for one week; this is the only time of my life for which I cannot account. How many times can one beat the odds? I survived the typhoid! It felt good to be alive and to have survived once again to face a hopefully better future.

The Canoe

> "God gives every bird its food, but he does not throw it into the nest." – Josiah Gilbert Holland (1819-81)

Once sufficiently recovered from typhoid and able to continue my homeward journey, I had to walk another 80 kilometres from Halberstadt to Magdeburg. Magdeburg was founded in the ninth century on the river Elbe, which then was the frontier between Germany and the Slavic lands. In April 1945, just a few days before the end of the war, 65 per cent of this once beautiful medieval city was unnecessarily destroyed by the Allied bomber command. It had become again the border between East and West. Most of the city was situated in the American occupied part of Germany and only a few suburbs on the east bank of the Elbe were in the Russian Zone. The many bridges over the Elbe were destroyed, except for one bridge that was the official gateway into the Russian Zone.

I fronted up with my American letter requesting permission to cross the bridge, but it produced nothing but a very decisive *"Nyet"* from the Russian border guard. A German man who had been hovering around approached me and offered to bring me across the river Elbe at night by canoe. Payment of the fare had to be made in $US. I explained to him that I did not have any US dollars. After some negotiations, we settled on fifteen loaves of bread. First, I had to find shelter for a few days, as it was quite a project to get the required bread together.

The few Jews of Magdeburg who had survived provided free temporary accommodation for Jewish Holocaust survivors in an old rundown building. In charge was a kindly elderly man, whose treatment in the camps had left him incontinent. The front of his pants was wet from time to time and he always smelt strongly of urine. I did not intend to stay there for one minute longer than it would take me to get my loaves of bread together. At the end of the war bread was scarce, and bakers who had bread for sale only sold one loaf per customer per day. Long queues of people always waited patiently outside the bakery stores until the last loaf had gone. The grapevine kept people in the know which baker, in what suburb, had bread available for sale. It was a daunting task to queue all day for bread in various suburbs of the city to get my fifteen loaves together. My typhoid-drawn face may have been of help to me, as it engendered sympathy. After a few days, I had succeeded in accumulating the fifteen loaves and I was ready to revisit my ferryman.

I waited for him in the street where we had first met, and we fixed a moonless night for the illegal river crossing. I had to hand over the bread first. After having received the bread he disappeared and he said that he would be back soon. Could I trust him? He did return after a short time and led me to the river's edge.

We took cover under a bush where he had already hidden his canoe. American soldiers drove up and down the western riverbank, but they turned a blind eye. Russian searchlights were shining across the river from the eastern bank. My canoe friend checked on the time. "Let's go," he said. We ran to the river's edge, jumped into the canoe, and he paddled across like a champion. The searchlights seemed to avoid us and with great precision we arrived on the other side of the river a long way down-tream near a bush. He shouted at me: "Out, run to the bush." I asked him: "What next?" but he was already on his way back across the river. I ran towards the bush and was received by two Russian soldiers who lay in wait for mc. "Watch?" they asked. I did not own a watch. They opened my rucksack that contained all my earthly belongings, and they carefully searched through it all, but could not find anything that was of commercial interest to them. They were most unhappy with the result of their search and looked disappointed. Then they took me to the *Kommandantura* where I had to sleep the night in its surrounding garden under the stars.

Next morning I was ordered to go to Berlin and to report to a "Displaced Persons Camp" in the American Sector of this city. Berlin is situated 140 kilometres east of Magdeburg, a relatively short walk compared with my previous travels. The railway started to run again in some places and I had perfected my technique of begging a free ride from kindly people. So I got to Berlin in a reasonably short time, walking some of the way, hitchhiking on railway engines, even getting a lift on a hearse and so on. The driver of the hearse found it strange that I was prepared to keep company with a dead body. Little did he know that the dying and the dead had been my most regular company during the past several years.

Breslau was still 350 kilometres southeast from Berlin, and the order from the Russian soldiers to report to West Berlin was not part of my plan. Jews have been called a race, a religious community, a people and a nation. We may be all that, but first and foremost we are a community, sharing a common history and a common fate. Persecution and anti-Semitism have welded us together into a community of fate and have created an otherwise unlikely affinity between the simple black-skinned Jews of Abyssinia, and the professional most sophisticated Jews of Europe and USA.

It was therefore only natural that I looked for temporary shelter and help from the remnants of the East Berlin Jewish community. At that time, everything happened in the one-time Jewish Aged Home in Iranische Strasse 3, which was right opposite the large Jewish hospital. Sabbath services were held there and temporary accommodation for Jewish survivors was granted. Some like me were moving east, others west and just a few had the courage to settle again in post-war Berlin and try to rebuild this community. My days were spent at railway stations and shunting yards, searching for a train to take me to Breslau. It was a hopeless task. The Russians were dismantling the second rail track, taking the rails, sleepers and rail bolts to Russia. I slept one night in an enclosed rail truck loaded with railway bolts destined for the Soviet Union. I awoke early the next morning as the train had already started to move, hopefully east towards Breslau.

It was a short-lived pleasure. I was chased off the rail truck in Guben 100 kilometres south-east of Berlin. I felt sore from lying and sitting on steel bolts for twenty-four hours and needed Russian papers to get to Breslau. East of the river Elbe during the Cold War, the Americans were the enemy. Perhaps, I could walk the 220 kilometres to Breslau over the only functioning bridge in this area. I tried to cross this bridge over the river Neisse into what was now Poland. A Soviet *Kommandatura* was on one side and a Polish soldier on the other side guarded the bridge. I asked the Russian officer for a pass. At that time, my knowledge of Russian was next to nil. "What was I?" "*Evrem* (Jew)," I said. He was not interested. "Where did I want to go?" I showed him Breslau on his map, which already had its new Polish name "Wrocław" on it. He seemed relieved to have solved his problem and gave me a pass, stating my nationality as *Polski Evrem* (Polish Jew). Full of hope I walked over the bridge, but the Polish border guards sent me back.

Jews were never very welcome in that country. After World War II, Jews who had escaped from Poland to Russia returned to try and pick up the threads of life, and many settled in Silesia. Despite an official non-racial policy of the communist government, cases of persecution of Jews by Poles occurred frequently. The religious anti-Semitism led to a pogrom in Kielce in 1946, where 43 Holocaust survivors were killed by a mob. This incident in turn led to a general exodus of most of the surviving Jews from Poland, especially after 1956, when the Gomułka government allowed Jews to emigrate.

I had to hitchhike back to Berlin, and spent a few more nights in the Jewish Aged Home to get some food and to regain my strength. During the day, it was back to the shunting yards looking for trains to Breslau. The Russians confiscated German furniture and railed them as booty to their homes in the Soviet Union. The stations were full of such trains. I hid inside a wardrobe standing on an open rail truck. It was midsummer and I did not know how much longer I could stand the heat in this confined space. This time I was lucky. The train started moving. I carefully opened the door to find that the door of the wardrobe opposite mine also opened and there we were, facing each other, two illegal travellers.

Shortly after the war, for both Poles and Russians, Germans were often free game, and being unable to tell my story in their language could have had severe consequences. We had travelled together for a few hours and not a single word had been spoken. When necessary, we peed off the moving train at opposite ends of the rail truck.

Suddenly the train stopped. Russian soldiers boarded it, asking for papers. Most of the hitchhikers had American, Polish or German papers. Consequently, they were led away by the Russian soldiers and forced to do some urgent work. I showed my Russian pass. They looked at it, said *"Chorosho"* (good) and left me on the train. As the train moved on, a mean-looking guy jumped on my rail truck. He was a travelling companion I could have well done without. I tried to keep awake, but exhaustion overtook me and I fell asleep, as always putting my head on my rucksack. When I awoke, it was already daylight. The train had stopped at the outskirts of Breslau. My travelling companion had disappeared, and with him my rucksack.

Now, all I owned was what I wore. I walked the last twenty kilometres back to the place of my birth, past dead horses on both sides of the road. Soldiers were removing landmines, and workers shovelled the rubble of the destroyed city off the road. I was no longer burdened by any earthly possessions. The unique experience derived from the persecution of Jews by the Third Reich was the only asset I had left, on which to build a future beyond survival.

The End of the Beginning

> "Men are what their mothers made them." – Ralph Waldo Emerson (1803-82)

The streets leading into the city of Breslau were lined with ruins and rubble. The ruins on the side of the road brought back many memories. I passed the large Jewish cemetery in the suburb of Cosel. During the last days of war, the Jews of Breslau had to share this burial ground with Jewish men who had died in the nearby labour camps and with SS soldiers who were killed in action when trying to defend *Festung Breslau* ("Fortress-Breslau") against the Russian Army during the last days of the Third Reich. No other suitable burial ground could be found for them. What separated us in life had vanished and the wisdom of the 24th Psalm became apparent: "The earth is God's and all its fullness, the world and all that dwell therein."

There was a sign on the cemetery wall with a warning not to enter it, because landmines had not yet been cleared. I would have dearly liked to visit my grandparents' graves, but it was not worth taking the risk. The administration building of the cemetery in which I'd been hospitalised before deportation had been reduced to rubble.

Next, I passed the abattoirs where Jews used to queue up to purchase meat. The abattoir's retail shop used to sell inferior meat to the poor for greatly reduced prices. When meat rationing was introduced, this shop would sell double the quantity of meat as was printed on the ration coupon. For Jews to be able to survive, the quantity of food was more important than quality and so most of us frequented this shop.

The picture theatre where my friends and I went, after having removed the yellow star, was still standing. It was a sad reminder of my friend Hans, whom I last saw in this theatre the day before he drowned. He was only thirteen years old and he was not spared to survive the Holocaust. Many more houses along the street leading into the city were destroyed than had been left standing, and the prospect of finding our last dwelling intact became more and more remote as I approached the city centre.

Three months had passed since I had left Neudorf in May 1945 and started this obstacle journey to Breslau. Not a single day had been wasted and yet it was now the middle of August. Would my battle to get back "home" have been in vain? I had been travelling at an increasing pace the closer I got to the end of my journey, but now that the final goal was almost in reach, I found myself slowing down with every step. More and more thoughts and questions arose in my mind and I became fearful that some of the answers to these questions might not be to my liking.

Would I find my mother still alive? Would she understand that my experiences since leaving home had changed me from an immature adolescent to a young man with a mind of his own? I suddenly realised that I had left school only three years ago, and had still so much to learn. Would it be possible for me to again become a schoolboy depending on the handout of a little pocket money from my parents? How would I cope having to abandon my independence and pick up the threads of the past? I had lost the key to the room we lived in and which my mother had asked me to look after when I left home. It had been stolen with the rucksack on the rail-truck before arriving back in Breslau. Had I also lost the key to the years of my childhood and youth, and would I be able to resume my old path of life? How odd, that since liberation I had worked so passionately to get back to this place, and now that I stood before the doorstep of my old home, I felt like a stranger. There was no way back for me. The past had already receded into history. There was only an uncertain way forward – a way leading to new struggles and the search for meaning in my life beyond survival.

The endless rows of destroyed houses gave way to a few buildings that had survived the Soviet conquest of the "Fortress-Breslau". One of the first houses still standing was the *Judenhaus* in Wallstrasse 31 from which I had been deported. The time for doubting and pondering had to come to an end. I resolutely entered the old building and went up the two flights of stairs. Nothing had changed. The little brass plate bearing our family name was still on the front door, as was the white star with the word *Jude* on it, which by order of the Gestapo had to be affixed to the entrance door of every Jewish dwelling.

I gently rang the bell. My mother opened the door and, after a short embrace, we greeted each other as though I had just returned home on the same day I had left. She was a most resilient woman. To me she appeared to be just the same as she was on the day that we said goodbye. She was wise enough not to comment on any changes she may have seen in me.

We were never a family that hid an inner emotional void behind drama and tears; on the contrary, it was an outer calm that often concealed a rich tapestry of inner thoughts and feelings. Life is not measured in time, but in the richness of the experiences within that allotted time. During the Holocaust, the events of one day exceeded the number of events and experiences other people went through during a lifetime. What one would have expected to be said at the time of our reunion required many years of storytelling; indeed, much of it has remained unsaid and will die within our memory.

The question has often been asked: Why did it take survivors of the Holocaust so long to tell their story and why did so many take their stories with them to the grave? The intensity of the experiences of these years of persecution took us into a world totally different from that into which we returned. There was much more that divided us than what we had in common with those who were not fellow travellers on our very special road through life.

I sat down in the one room that was once allotted to us by the Gestapo. My mother disappeared to tell our new Jewish Polish neighbours about my return. They returned with cake and real coffee, even with whipped cream, all things I had not been able to enjoy for years. I looked at mother, and could not help but notice that the Holocaust had taken its toll. She was only 41 years old, but it showed that she had been cheated out of the best years of her life.

Afternoon coffee was over, and we both wanted to know what had happened to the other since we were separated. Before talking about it, mother sent me to have a little rest. I fell asleep instantly and slept almost non-stop for 24 hours before we had gathered sufficient strength to be able to tell each other our respective stories.

Halka

> *"Cela va bien, la montagne est passée!"* (All went well, the mountain has been climbed over!) – Friedrich II's last words (17 August 1786)

It was a stroke of luck that on my return to Breslau I found my mother still alive. Her time in the "Fortress-Breslau" was no less hazardous than mine had been in the concentration camp. After Father and I had left Breslau in 1944, mother had stayed behind with the last 150 Jews of this community.

From January 1945 until the surrender of the city to the Russian Army on Sunday, 6 May 1945, Breslau stood under the political control of Gauleiter Karl August Hanke (1903-45). He was the man whom Hitler had appointed as Chief of the SS and the Police, in lieu of Heinrich Himmler in his political testament of 29 April 1945. Hanke's brutality was legendary, not only against Jews, but also against his fellow Germans. On 28 January 1945, he publicly executed the Deputy Lord Mayor of Breslau, Dr Wolfgang Spielhagen (1891-1945) for trying to save the beleaguered city from destruction by the Russians. In a public notice to the 200,000 remaining citizens of Breslau (there had been 720,000 in 1944), Hanke announced that he had personally ordered this execution and that "whosoever fears death with honour will die a death of shame". While executing others for lack of patriotism, he himself escaped, using one of the last planes from the "Fortress-Breslau" to the Sudetenland. Ironically, he was beaten to death by Czech partisans during the last days of the war. The battle to occupy the city by the Russian Army lasted from January to May 1945.

Hanke did not let his work to defend the city allow him to forget to deal with the remaining 100-150 Jews. Just before Breslau was totally encircled, he ordered the Gestapo to organise two final transports of Jews to the concentration camp Gross-Rosen. The first transport left Breslau and got to Gross-Rosen, but was redirected from there to the concentration camp of Bergen-Belsen. None of these deportees survived.

My mother, like all the remaining Jews, now had to work in the fortification of the city under constant artillery fire and air attacks. Shrapnel had hit one of our flatmates, Max Cohen. He was paralysed and heavily bleeding. My mother and his wife wheeled him on a handcart from hospital to hospital. The hospitals did not accept "non-Aryan" patients. He died on the cart and they had to bring his body home again. The two women buried him in the park opposite Wallstrasse 31. A young Jewish nurse who had looked after me in hospital before deportation, died from burst lungs caused from the air-pressure of a nearby exploding artillery shell.

The planned second transport of Jews could no longer leave the city, as by now it was completely encircled by the Russian Army. The last few Jews, including my mother, were put on a barge on the river Oder, with the intent to blow the barge up and sink it in the middle of the river. Russian air raids and artillery bombardment foiled this plan. Mother and the other Jewish people were sent home and ordered to report back again on the following day. Those who reported back were executed. Mother did not follow the order, but hid for the rest of the war in the rat-infested cellars of the partially destroyed houses of Breslau, with little to eat.

The war had ended for the world, but not for my mother. Until Father and I returned to Breslau, mother was still hiding at night in the cellar. She had experienced the entire war in Breslau, but the harassment by the Gestapo, the uncertainty of my father's and my fate after deportation, and her own planned deportation in the last days of the war, had taken its toll.

What was she hiding from? The Soviet Army had occupied Breslau, but this part of Germany had been promised to Poland after the war. The Poles were not willing to wait for this to be implemented in the distant future. They were impatient, and lacked faith in Stalin honouring his commitment. Ex-Polish partisans became the core from which developed the Polish militia and later became the Polish Army. Immediately after the war, Soviet troops and the Polish militia were fighting a private war in the streets of Breslau. They were fighting one another, as well as their once common enemy, the Germans. Heavy drinking and sexual frustration lead to looting and raping. Sir Antony Beevor in his book *Berlin: The Downfall 1945* estimates that at least two million German women were raped and that Russian women, who had just been liberated from German imprisonment, were not immune from rape either.

Most of the few German-Jewish women who had returned to or had remained in Breslau, could speak neither Polish nor Russian, and by the time they could offer explanations of their background, it was too late. Just days before I had arrived back home, the mother of a Jewish school friend who had survived the war and had just returned from Auschwitz was shot by a Russian soldier when she tried to resist rape.

There was no point in hiding from the reality of the situation any longer.

I had returned to a place that was no longer home. The city of my birth was 80 per cent destroyed. Strangers whose language I could not speak lived in it. Of the 27,000 Jews of this 900-year-old Jewish community, only 40 to 60 had returned to Breslau. Most had been murdered, and a few had been scattered throughout the world. We who had returned tried to rebuild the Jewish community, but it was of no use, as we had two handicaps in the now Polish Wrocław. We were both *Germans* and *Jews* to the new Polish citizens of this city. It was time to move on.

Despite the general destruction of the city, the old Opera House, where once the composers Carl Maria von Weber and Engelbert Humperdinck were musical directors, had survived the war. My parents and grandparents used to be subscribers to the opera season before 1933 and had spent many happy hours within its walls. It was reopened with the opera *Halka* by Stanisław Moniuszko, one of the few operas composed by a Polish composer. I went to hear it and loved the performance, especially after being starved for cultural events during the Hitler years.

On the way home, the Polish militia and Russian troops were having, as so often happened, a shoot-out in the streets. I did not have far to walk home and I tried to avoid trouble. No such luck! The Polish militia dragged me into their *Kommandantura.* They were hostile, choosing not to understand German. My identity pass issued by the Jewish community in Polish and Russian did not help matters. After some shouting and discussions, they sent me out into the dark night. They had been drinking heavily. Jews have always made good shooting targets, and I did not want to be one. I hid in the nearest ruin until things had quietened down, and then ran home, trying to keep looking around for snipers in four directions at once. This was not an isolated incident. I was lucky to survive it.

Every day busloads of Poles returned to Poland from Germany. Günter Singer (1922-89), the secretary of the small Jewish community who had survived Auschwitz, negotiated with these bus drivers to take us as return passengers back to Germany. Singer's young wife had been gassed in Auschwitz and he too was looking for a new beginning, away from the place that was full of painful memories.

We could only take two suitcases per person with us on the bus. This meant that we had to get rid of all surplus belongings. We flogged them off at the black market for German marks, a currency that was soon to be devalued. And so, the remnants of the Breslau German Jewish community ended up in Erfurt, the hometown of the bus company.

As we arrived in Erfurt, this city had just changed from American to Soviet occupation. The Americans pulled out of the province of Thuringia in exchange for the American sector of Berlin. In our desire to come to rest, we had failed to notice that we were now locked away behind the Iron Curtain. I never heard the opera *Halka* again, but the shooting incident after the opera performance was one of the catalysts that made me leave the city of my birth and that determined the future direction of my journey through life.

Porta Coeli

> "Knowing is not enough; we must apply. Willing is not enough; we must do." – Johann Wolfgang von Goethe (1749-1832)

The 500-kilometre bus ride from Breslau to Erfurt was quite an ordeal. The bus was an old worn-out Erfurt-City bus, not built for long-distance traffic. It was overloaded with too many passengers who were packed into the bus among the many suitcases. There was no chance to get comfortable and sleep. We arrived in Erfurt late at night, totally exhausted. We settled into a room in the Savoy, an old-fashioned, run-down inner city hotel which had seen better days. From 1933 until our arrival in Erfurt, the pattern of our life was reactive to the dictates of the authorities. Suddenly, we found ourselves in a hotel room having to become proactive again. Questions of "Where to live?" and "What to do with our lives?" had to be addressed.

The first job in the morning was to visit the city's accommodation office.

Erfurt had suffered little bomb damage during the war and therefore it had to accept refugees from the Eastern German provinces that had been annexed by Poland, as well as the inhabitants from bombed-out German cities. We were allocated to single furnished rooms in a luxurious apartment belonging to the May family. Officially, Mrs May was the sole occupier of the apartment. Mr May was listed as a missing German soldier and her only son had been killed in action at the Russian front.

She greeted our arrival with mixed feelings. She hoped that by taking a Jewish family into her home, she would be sheltered from having her nice home being requisitioned by the occupying Soviet Army. On the other hand, she had found comfort in her loneliness by having an affair and she was not sure how we would react to the frequent overnight stays of her friend. The matter got even more complicated when her husband returned home unexpectedly from a Soviet prisoner of war camp.

By that time, we had found a small unit of our own nearby. We had made good friends with Mrs May. We had helped her to get back to a normal life. Her friend had moved to West Germany, where he no doubt would have found some other lonely heart to comfort. The immediate post-war period was marked by a shortage of men, which led to many problems in personal relationships.

Erfurt was the home of Dr Diehl & Co, a large shoe factory that was once owned by Jews. During the war it produced boots for the German Army, and after the war it was commissioned to produce boots for the Soviet Army. It was also intended by the post-war administration to hand this company back to the rightful heirs of the original Jewish owners.

My father's managerial experience in the shoe industry made him the right candidate to become the administrator/manager of this enterprise. He started this job the day after our arrival. The company began to flourish, but the constant fight against corruption was endemic in the impoverished post-war Germany. One day when

Father had to supervise a delivery of boots to the Soviet Army, the army officer receiving the goods would deliberately miscount the number of boots to siphon some of them off for sale on the black market. My father made him count properly. The officer took out his revolver, pointed it at my father and asked him to count the boots his way. My father pointed a pen at the officer and said: "Take your choice. Either sign for the right quantity, or shoot."

This incident coincided with a policy change of the governments of the East German provinces. These communist governments proclaimed that all capitalists, whether Jewish or Aryan, had acquired their property by "stealing" it from the people. Consequently, such property had to be returned to the people and not to any past or present capitalists. Therefore, all major firms in East Germany became *Volkseigene Betriebe* (companies owned by the people).

Father used this change in government policy to resign from the shoe company, but they would not let a man with his talents go. He was appointed *Regierungsrat* (government department head) of the Department for Economic Planning of the East German State of Thuringia. He held this position until he defected, first to West Berlin (October 1950) and later to Australia (February 1951).

I had decided to study medicine and this required hard work without an end in sight. What prompted me to make this decision is not clear to me. It probably was more subconscious than deliberate. Was it because a relative had left with us his medical books or because I had been surrounded by death and the dying for years? Did medicine as a profession that tries to maintain life attract me to it? Or could it have been the desire for recognition and status in life after being downgraded during the Hitler years? The reason for this decision is now of little importance, but it served me well, as it taught me how to work hard and to always learn whatever was on offer.

At the time, I was sixteen-and-a-half years old; my schooling had stopped when I was thirteen. I needed to pass my normal German *Abitur* (final high school examination) for entrance into university studies, including the "Latinum" and "Graecum" (high standard in Latin and Greek) that was required for the study of medicine. I had eighteen months to achieve that objective to pass the *Abitur* at the appropriate age. The time in labour and concentration camps had taught me how to manage with only five hours sleep per night and how to dispense with the luxury of weekends and holiday breaks. The only diversion from my studies were violin lessons at the Thuringian State Conservatorium and acting as relief cantor for synagogue services.

I went with my father to meet the headmaster of the state secondary school called *Oberschule zur Himmelspforte.* The school had been established in 1461 with the Latin name *Porta Coeli* and it prided itself on having had Martin Luther (1483-1546) as one of its pupils. The headmaster Dr Franke had served during World War I in the German Army, like my father, which became an instant subject for conversation and helped to break down barriers. Franke organised private lessons for me with every class teacher after school, to catch up on the gaps in my knowledge. He told me that it required Prussian discipline to achieve my objective. In addition to Prussian discipline, I had the firm Jewish commitment for learning and understanding. It was one of my biggest battles in life, as in addition to Greek, Latin, English and French, I had to learn Russian, a compulsory subject in the Russian Occupied Zone of Germany. In the end, it was all worth it. I passed my *Abitur* at the right age in the normal manner "cum laude".

My school mates were normal German boys, keen to kick a football, play *skat* (a German national card game), engage in silly pranks and foster old friendships going back to their time in the Hitler Youth. I was the only Jew in the school, an exhibition piece that was not at all like the stereotype Jew they had been taught about during the Third Reich. Yet I was very different to them, as a good part of my childhood and adolescence had been lost in the Holocaust. They helped me to rediscover some of it and they taught me that each day is the first day of the rest of one's life. To earn their respect, I had to pull my weight in the football team, be the lead violin in the school orchestra and write articles in the school magazine. My studying time was shortened by being laid up for a month with viral hepatitis, which was brought to Germany by the Russian Army and which had reached epidemic proportions at that time.

You can find at least 48 hours in every day provided you try hard enough. Indeed, I did find these extra hours and I used them to look for interesting places and people. There was the reopening of the German National Theatre in Weimar with a performance of Goethe's *Faust* by Germany's top actors. There were the many visits to the Wartburg where Luther translated the Bible into German and where the painter Moritz von Schwind painted all the German minstrels, except the German Jewish troubadour Süsskind von Trimberg.

I took a rather depressed Jewish friend along to the Wartburg, and as we ascended the tower of this medieval fortress, he froze in a fit of agoraphobia. It took a long time and lots of persuasion to move him back out of the tower into the open. His father, who had returned from Auschwitz and attempted to enter his onetime country home, was shot by Soviet soldiers who occupied this building and who thought this to be the best way to deal with the unwanted intruder.

The war had caused many human tragedies. The charming young daughter of one of my father's business associates would disappear quite frequently for some days into the country. She was waiting for her fiancée to return from a Soviet prisoner of war camp, which he did. But he left her heartbroken as quickly as he came. A Russian soldier had raped her and the mysterious trips to the country were visits to her resulting little son. The fiancé could not accept the boy; the Russian soldier had returned to his family in the Soviet Union and she was left a single mum. Neither she nor the boy found acceptance by a population with little sympathy for, or understanding of, her plight.

Not far from the Weimar of Goethe and Schiller was the Weimar of the concentration camp of Buchenwald. My father's cousin was brutalised there in 1938, together with thousands of German Jews. The left-wing political parties in the Soviet Zone of Germany were determined to make Buchenwald the national shrine of East Germany. They rewrote history. The Jewish suffering in this camp was marginalised and all persecution by Hitler was politicised. Little did I know at the time that the Soviet military administration in Germany had established in August 1945 in Buchenwald, a *Speziallager* (specialised camp) in which 23,000 adversaries of communist rule were receiving "special treatment" and of whom only 4000 survived. This is testimony to the truth in the saying: "Politics is like breeding pigs. The pigsties are always the same; it is only the pigs that change."

My school days were troubled by two groups of people trying to exert political pressure on me. First there were the communists. On 22 April 1946, two political parties in the Soviet Zone of Germany amalgamated. The KPD (Communist Party of Germany) and the SPD (Socialist Party of Germany) united into the SED (Socialist Unity Party of Germany). The SED soon marginalised all other political parties and became the dominant political force, thus making East Germany a Soviet-style political dictatorship. The SED developed a youth wing called FDJ (Free German Youth) and I was regularly pressured to join it to be able to advance in my studies. I resisted and never became a member of the FDJ, but it became more and more obvious to me that unless I was willing to sell my soul to the East German state, my days of higher education in East Germany would be numbered.

The second group pressuring me was the Zionist lobby, which tried to convince Holocaust survivors that the right place for them after Auschwitz was Israel, the yet-to-be-established Jewish state. Hitler branded us a "race apart" from the peoples among whom we lived. I was not prepared to give Hitler a posthumous victory and abandon the Jewish concept of universalism. The Nazi dogma that the bond that keeps a nation together is *Blut und Boden* (blood and soil) may apply to a nation, but at the same time it is the ferment from which hate and war between the nations emanate. My common bond with my fellow Jews is that we have walked the same road through history, experienced the same persecution over the centuries, and have a joint commitment to improving the human condition in our own time. I could not commit to withdraw into the cloistered imaginary security of a Jewish state. To be a Jew after the Holocaust meant to me to re-enter the family of man, regardless of whether we were welcome or merely tolerated.

I am aware that the State of Israel has become an historic necessity for all who had prayed for millennia to return to the place of the genesis of Jewish life. It is of even greater need for Jews for whom persecution had not yet ended, and who had nowhere else to go. In 1936, Chaim Weizmann declared before the Peel Commission: "For persecuted Jews the world is divided into places where Jews can't live and into others where they can't go". The State of Israel has changed this, and it requires help from every Jew for its continued existence for as long as mankind chooses to live within the confines of nation states.

My deep concern about Israel is that the world will continue to question the legitimacy of a Jewish presence in this tiny piece of land, where every place has a Hebrew name, and every stone tells of this people's presence there throughout history. I can also well understand the feeling of sadness and loss of Palestinians who have been displaced from their former homes in the State of Israel, as I am a "displaced person" myself. Millions of people have been displaced and resettled as the consequence of World War II, and through the self-determination of countries which once were part of colonial empires.

I have great concern that it is taking the Arab world so long to take into their lands the relatively small number of Palestinians who are still living in refugee camps under harsh conditions. I also watch with grave concern the growth of Jewish religious fundamentalism and extreme nationalism. Already in 1917, the lawyer and political analyst of the *Manchester Guardian,* Harry Sacher (1882-1971), a close collaborator of Chaim Weizmann, wrote: "I do not want to see that we treat the Arabs like the Poles treat the Jews ... We need a great and constructive program to counter the rifles and machine guns of our Hurrah-patriots."

When I completed my *Abitur,* and being a "victim of fascism", I was offered a choice between the universities of Jena and the Humboldt University in Berlin for my studies in medicine. I needed time to make the choice between studying medicine in Germany, or emigrating to Israel or elsewhere in the world. Berlin was the place to go, as the wall was not yet built, and I could commence my studies and cross the border before the Iron Curtain would finally close on me.

I left Erfurt with regret, as it was there that I had learnt again that to be a Jew demands to be a complete human being. I have nothing but pleasant memories of my time in Thuringia, this *Green Heart of Germany.* Before leaving, I wandered for the last time through the forest to the Gickelhahn Mountain where the ageing Goethe wrote this beautiful poem:

Wanderer's Night Song

Above all summits it is calm.
On all the tree-tops you feel scarcely a breath.
The birds in the forest are silent.
Just wait; soon you shall rest as well.

I was hoping to come to rest after the turmoil of the Third Reich, but this was still a long way off.

The Girl with One Leg

> "I can only think of music as something inherent in every human being – a birthright. Music coordinates mind, body and spirit."
> – Yehudi Menuhin (1916-99)

Berlin, after the war, was a heap of rubble. The Western sectors of the city started to rebuild and consumer goods were again on offer, but you needed West German marks to purchase them. The Eastern sector where I had to live was still very drab, and food and merchandise were scarce, rationed, and of poor quality. However, the "HO Stores" sold goods that were rationed in this sector at ten times the normal price. The HO was a monument to the failure of socialism in East Germany, as these stores catered for the SED (Socialist Unity Party of Germany) fat-cats and excluded the average citizens who could not afford to shop in these stores. The East German mark exchanged against the West German mark at seven to one, which made participation in the life of West Berlin prohibitive. Trams and buses would stop at the border between the East and West sector, and as you crossed the border you had to buy another ticket in West German currency. Rebuilding of the city was slow, and accommodation was at a premium.

I was lucky to get a small room in the *Jüdisches Alters und Kinderheim,* Moltkestrasse 8-10 in Niederschönhausen. I shared this room with Roland Rothschild, an apprentice chef in the Jewish hospital. He was a nice guy but he loved to play pop music, which made it hard at times to concentrate on studying. Life in Berlin was exciting and stimulating, especially for a university student. There was Max Karl Ernst Ludwig Planck (1858-1947), whose quantum mechanics had contributed so much to the understanding of the atom, exploring in a series of lectures the relationship between human knowledge and ethical behaviour. These lectures were published in East Germany in a superb little volume called *Die Aufgaben und*

Grenzen der exakten Wissenschaft (The Tasks and Limitations of Science). It was a great pity that the book had so little effect on the world. It may have averted Pol Pot's Killing Fields, the massacres in Rwanda, ethnic cleansing in Yugoslavia, and the religious wars in the Middle East.

The Anatomical Institute in the Karlstrasse also had its fascination. There was a large collection of the brains of important people of the past preserved in glass containers. This collection had been put together by Rudolf Ludwig Karl Virchow (1821-1902), who proved that the size and weight of the brain is not related to its intellectual output. His son, the anatomist Hans Virchow (1852-1940), who also worked there, was not happy about women being allowed to study medicine. In Hans Virchow's view, the practice of medicine was a sacred task reserved for the superior intelligence of the male of the species. He kept the male and female students apart in separate dissection halls, and used the women to chart the details of the many small muscles on the spine. He thought this tedious task was women's work.

I joined the small Jewish Students Group in Berlin. It was of multicultural background, and deeply committed to learning and catching up on missed opportunities. We were united in showing a visiting American Jewish psychologist, who wanted to study us Holocaust survivors, the cold shoulder. He wanted to know: What effect had the Holocaust had on our minds? How could we live and study again in Germany after Hitler? For us, he suffered from an American obsession called *Psychology.* Our problems were our own, and we had to overcome them and get on with our lives.

We were greatly divided when Yehudi Menuhin came to Berlin in 1947 to give a concert in the *Admiralspalast* with the Berlin Philharmonic Orchestra conducted by Wilhelm Furtwängler. After a year's prohibition from conducting, Furtwängler was finally "denazified" and reinstated as musical director of the Berlin Philharmonic Orchestra. Yehudi Menuhin had come to Berlin to join him in a concert to play Beethoven's D

Major Violin Concerto. The Berlin Jewish Students Group decided to boycott this concert. It took some soul-searching to find my own answer. Was it appropriate to boycott Beethoven because he was a German, as revenge for Mendelssohn and Mahler being banned in the Third Reich, because they were *racially* Jews? Was the attempt by Menuhin to build bridges after the dark years of the Hitler era a sign of weakness? I admired the courage of Menuhin to point towards a new beginning, at a time when wounds still had to heal. I had to be there, had to be counted.

The concert that brought together the greatest German music played by the great Jewish violinist and the great German conductor was an experience of religious intensity. It brought together in the ruins of Berlin German families who, with few exceptions, had lost family members on the battlefield or in the bombed-out German cities, and just a few Jewish survivors who had lost so many of their own in the extermination camps of Europe. That night we listened together to the great music of this concerto, which portrays the peace enjoyed by a happier generation, and which gave the concerto the name Beethoven's 10th Symphony. Together we experienced the world as it was, and the world as it could have been.

We were left with the challenge to work towards rebuilding and reconciliation. I had to suffer the abuse of some of my Jewish fellow students for having broken rank. It was nothing compared with the treatment meted out to Menuhin. The American authorities arranged a Furtwängler/Menuhin concert for the displaced persons who stayed in the Berlin Düppel Centre. It was planned for the Tivoli Theatre, with a seating capacity of well over a thousand. Fewer than 50 people attended. I was reminded of the saying by the British Reform Rabbi Lionel Blue: "Jews are just like everyone else, only more so."

In Max Reinhardt's Deutsches Theater the great actor Alfred Berliner, who had survived living underground, played again to packed and enthusiastic houses. In 1964, the German writer Herbert Freeden (Friedenthal, 1909-2003) wrote a book, *Jewish*

Theatre in Nazi Germany. He describes in this book the grand opening of the *Kulturbund* (Association of Jewish Artists) in Berlin in 1933 with Lessing's classical play *Nathan der Weise,* in which the actor Alfred Berliner played the lead. Freeden further comments in this book, "What an hour of bitter triumph. A Jew, whose wife and family were murdered, proclaims the message of tolerance and humanity in the ruins of post-war Berlin!"

One day, the university closed for a day to give all students the opportunity to listen to the Russian biologist Trofim Denisovich Lysenko (1898-1976) and to learn about his new method for getting a greater yield from a cereal harvest by replanting plants deeper into the soil. It seemed to work in the laboratory, but he forgot to tell the world how to pay for the labour required to replant the world's grain harvest each year.

Perhaps the most lasting impression came from my anatomical studies. Eight students were assigned to one cadaver. There was no shortage of cadavers so shortly after the war. Our group of eight was lucky. We were given the body of a beautiful young woman. She had lost one leg, and the neat stitches of the amputation operation had not yet healed. She was not a virgin, so someone must have loved her. Her face reminded me of the death mask of *"L'inconnue de la Seine"* (the sculpture of a girl who had drowned and whose body was pulled out of the Seine River) which adorned so many walls of European homes.

We worked on the girl's body for a good part of the year, systematically dismantling it and placing it bit by bit into an empty drum provided, so that it could be all buried together after we had completed our dissection exercise. There was no other person whose every part of the body I knew in such detail, and at the same time there was no other person about whom I knew so very little. Who was she? What was her life all about? Why did the mystique of this most beautiful face and body stay with me after we had destroyed it? How could we know so much about that part of her body which was the same as everyone else's and nothing at all about the part of her that made her different and a unique human being? Why did we respectfully collect each bit of her flesh and bone to be buried together, when, in the extermination camps of Europe, the ashes of millions of Jews, Gypsies, men, women and children were all mixed up in a common grave?

The rabbi and philosopher Dr Leo Baeck taught in Berlin about the ways of the Jewish mind. It does not follow the Greek principle of theses and antitheses, nor the Christian teaching of Christ and anti-Christ. Contradictory manifestations such as light and darkness, good and evil, time and eternity, body and soul, men and women, do not lack the reality of being, because they offend the man-made logical rules of cause and effect.

The acknowledgement of the "twinfold", or should we say "multifold" nature of this world does not diminish, but adds to its meaning. While I knew to perfection the physical reality of this woman with the one leg, the knowledge of the other half of her real being, may I call it her soul, was totally denied to me.

Likewise, in Berlin, I was familiar with the rubble of this great city and lived amidst the ashes of millions of destroyed lives. However, to fully understand the other part of this *twinfold* reality, the innermost soul of the oppressor and the oppressed, the victor and vanquished, was denied to me.

Indeed, to me the fascination with the Holocaust is that it was not committed by savages about whom one does not care, but by one of the world's most educated and cultured nations. In my daily life, I had to discover, again and again, that professors at the Berlin University to whom I owed so much, and fellow students who had become close and caring friends, were bystanders, or even were involved in the atrocities of the past. I needed the distance of time and space from Europe, the birthplace of my own soul, to find meaning in the chaos of the colourful tapestry of history that occurred during the years of my struggle for survival. Three events helped me to decide to move on.

On 24 June 1948 Berlin became an island amid the East German state, sustained only by the "Berlin Airlift". My father was more and more pressured to identify with the government of East Germany. A new academic subject was made compulsory for all branches of studies at the Berlin Humboldt University: "The Social and Political Problems of the Present". This subject was designed to separate the true believers in the new East Germany from those "not worthy" of enjoying the privilege of higher education.

Our family had stayed in Nazi Germany because we left the decision to emigrate too late. I was not going to make the same mistake again and become trapped in the communist world. My only chance to leave Berlin quickly was emigration to Australia. I left the DDR *(Deutsche Demokratische Republik)* illegally and secretly. The choice was between betraying the confidence of my newly acquired German friends, or to betray the call of my conscience. The decision was impulsive and instinctive. I am still left with the doubt: "Did I neglect my duty as a Jew to teach in post-war Germany by example, and do I now merely soothe my conscience by writing and moralising about these times from the distance, years after the events?"

I belong to a generation that can tell so many stories about suffering and happiness. A generation schooled in disappointments and persecuted human beings who survived by dreaming of a better world. As I wake up from the dark of this night, I must express my gratitude for having survived, and try to point the way towards a better future.

Hebrew Lessons

"I don't think of all the misery, but of the beauty that still remains." - Anne Frank (1929-45)

After the war in Berlin, I used to wear a small silver Star of David in my lapel. Most Jewish survivors did. At the time, we believed that we wore it to show that we again could feel proud to be Jews, and that Hitler's yellow star was never a burden. Most of us still remembered the leading article in the *Jüdische Rundschau* during the Hitler years by its editor-in-chief Robert Weltsch: *"Tragt ihn mit Stoltz, den gelben Fleck!"* (Wear it with pride, the yellow badge!) But was this the true reason or did we in fact wear it to distance ourselves from the Germans among whom we lived? Was the real reason to remind our German neighbours of their guilt towards us? It still troubles me greatly to this day, that at the time I blindly followed the herd instinct and I failed to comprehend that being Jewish requires one to have understanding, to have compassion and to teach by example. Being Jewish does not occur by being labelled a Jew.

I should have known better, as during the years of persecution I had soaked up Jewish knowledge, learnt Hebrew, Torah, Talmud, the writings of Maimonides, Moses Mendelssohn, Franz Rosenzweig, Martin Buber and Leo Baeck, to mention just a few. Living in the Jewish Children's Home made me aware that the few children who had survived the Holocaust needed to be taught about Judaism, so I offered my services to act as a teacher at the religious school of the Berlin Jewish community. I was ready to offer a rabbinic curriculum to young people who did not need to be force-fed with 3000 years of Jewish thoughts and history, but who instead required to have their lives normalised.

I remember a little Jewish girl from the Children's Home who was often sent home from school with a note that she again had stolen lunch from other children. She had lived underground during the war and her only way of survival was to steal food. Now it was difficult to reprogram her and make her understand that times had changed and that stealing food was no longer acceptable.

One day the Jewish community took me up on my offer to teach. The man who phoned me said that my study of medicine, and my knowledge of Judaism, would make me most suited to teach a bedridden spastic child who lived in a cellar beneath a partially bombed-out building near the ruins of a synagogue in Oranienburger Strasse. I agreed grudgingly, because I felt that my talents were under-utilised and wasted, teaching just one girl instead of a school class.

On my first visit, I was greeted by an endless flow of words from the mother of the child. She told me that she was a prostitute by profession and by using these special talents in the concentration camp on the SS, she survived. The spastic child was the result of the attention given to her by an SS officer who used her for sexual gratification, but who also protected her.

She explained, that as she, the mother, was Jewish, according to Jewish Orthodox tradition, the child was also

Jewish. She also assured me that God had made the child spastic to punish her. She called the father of the child "The Producer". The girl was totally bedridden, and the dreary cellar room was her world. She had great difficulties to control her hand movements and her speech was slurred. It took me quite a while to understand her. Her eyes were bright and she was intelligent, eager to learn and of an unbelievably cheerful disposition. I came to teach her the *history* of Judaism; she taught me the *essence* of Judaism. Where was I going to begin? I remembered the Hebrew name of the first book of the Torah, *Bereshith* (the Beginning). That was the place to start. I told her the stories of Genesis and I asked her to make drawings about them for the next lesson. It did not occur to me that she might not be able to draw too well and even less did I understand that, despite her handicaps, her determination to succeed would produce the most colourful and meaningful drawings. We talked about the legends of Genesis and discovered together the great human insights in the stories of the Torah.

Adam and Eve facing the hardships that comes with knowledge; Abraham, unwilling to accept that there should not be a single kindly soul in Sodom and Gomorrah; Jacob, comparing life to a ladder standing on earth and reaching towards Heaven; Moses finding wisdom in solitude before the burning bush and on the peak of the barren Mount Sinai and finally wandering off on his own towards his Maker. At each lesson, I learnt more than I taught.

I also acquired a large circle of non-Jewish friends. This was not difficult to accomplish. After 1945 it was the in-thing for German non-Jews to mix with Jews, and as they had been brainwashed for the twelve years of the Third Reich that Jews are the scum of the earth, even the worst of us was a pleasant surprise to them. A special friendship had developed with my seven fellow anatomy students. We had to study and dissect the same cadaver, which meant that we had to keep a roster for covering it around the clock with wet formaldehyde sheets to prevent it from drying out.

One of the students was Mrs St..., a beautiful and charming young German woman who had married a Polish Jew who was never home with her and who seemed to play the field. We mostly met at her home for shared meals and joint study sessions. Then there was Miss B... who like me came from Erfurt. She had chosen to study in Berlin to be able to meet her boyfriend, who was studying law in Hamburg. This was the only way these two could meet, otherwise being parted by living in the different Soviet and British Occupation Zones of Germany. We usually went by train together for breaks to see our respective families in Erfurt. Most trains at the time were overcrowded and did not yet have any glass in the window frames. Sometimes we had to travel on the platform between two rail wagons, and as the rail engines were fuelled with lignite, the sparks flying along the train made us arrive at the end of the journey with sore eyes that required washing out for some days.

Another Berlin friend was Hans, whose father had been killed in the war, and who lived with his mother in a small apartment. The mother was a very possessive woman, who never missed an opportunity to let Hans know that were it not for her hard work he would be unable to study medicine. We were all a family substitute, a haven away from the strains and stresses in his home. We met before lectures to check notes on what had not been fully understood, and went to the theatre, opera and museums together. Whenever one or the other failed to turn up, we were concerned about what might have happened to them.

Dark clouds of Cold War politics started to cast their shadows over the joy of my student life. In December 1946, the Washington treaty decided on the economic unification of the Western Zones of Germany, which led to the decision in April 1948 to establish a West German State with its own currency. The reaction of the Russian Zone was to tighten up on its citizens, who defected by the thousands to the West. Planning commenced to establish the "German Democratic Republic" (DDR) in the East, and it was obvious that this state had to stop the disappearance of its citizens into the West.

My father had to make his home available for meetings of the Stasi (the secret police of East Germany). He would not cooperate in the meetings that took place in his own home, and he bought himself a large Alsatian dog called Axel to make the visitors as uncomfortable as possible. He left the visitors alone in our home, which was a risky thing to do, as they could have planted incriminating material against him and given him the *Special Treatment* in nearby Buchenwald.

It was suggested to me that, after having studied in Berlin for some semesters, it now would be best for my study program to follow the German custom and continue studying at the University of Leipzig. On 20 March 1948 the last session of the Allied Control Commission took place.

It was time for me to leave Germany. The price was high, as it was the end of my dream to make medicine my profession. I had to establish a fake address in West Berlin, cease going home to Erfurt to see my parents, use a pseudonym when writing to them and work hard on my emigration. I wanted to go to the USA, but so did everybody else. As time was of the essence, I settled on my second preference and I went to Australia.

I could not trust a soul in the Stasi-controlled Soviet Zone, and so I left Berlin University without deregistering and left my friends without telling them of my plan. I also could not take the risk of telling the mother of the spastic child, who was a rather loose cannon and a common woman, that the Hebrew lessons were coming to an end.

At the last lesson, I felt like Esau, who sold his birthright for a potage of lentils. I was about to betray the faith and trust this sensitive young soul had given to me, for the material opportunity that lay before me in faraway Australia. She was one of my great teachers, who made me always search for joy and light, even in the darkness of night, and for that I shall always remember her with deep gratitude.

The Princess

> "The Ghetto outlook divided this Universe into two: This world for the Gentile and the next world for the Jew." – David Ben Gurion (David Grün, 1886-1954)

Almost every day, I travelled by underground to the offices of HIAS (Hebrew Immigrant Aid Society) and IRO (International Refugee Organisation) in the outer Berlin suburb of Berlin-Zehlendorf, to further my planned emigration to Australia. There were always long queues of refugees in these offices, waiting to get away from Europe and to look for their fortunes in different parts of the world. To achieve my objective became more and more difficult, as on 24 June 1948 Berlin had become an island. The Soviet authorities had stopped all traffic by rail, road and waterways into the Western sectors of the city. Until 30 September 1949, West Berlin was kept alive by the "Airlift". Planes arrived and left every few minutes, feeding and sustaining West Berlin.

At that time, the movement of people for private travel in and out of Berlin was of low priority. The atmosphere in the immigration offices was unpleasant, as the pressure of work made the officers bureaucratic and surly, and their clients impatient and aggressive. To get a passage on an ocean liner to Australia was difficult, and there was a long waiting list. I had only East German currency, which was not acceptable in the West, and that made me dependent on aid organisations advancing me the required money.

It became increasingly urgent for me to leave Berlin to avoid being locked away behind the Iron Curtain. My best option was to move to Paris and to wait there until a passage became available on either a French or an Italian passenger liner. In August 1949, all was ready for me to leave Berlin. I could only take one large case, accommodating four changes of clothes, one suit, one outfit for every day and my favourite books. These were all my earthly belongings. The clothes were lovingly marked by my mother with my initials "KA" and the few books were a strange collection of essential reading: Goethe's *Faust, Atlas of Human Anatomy* by Rauber-Kopsch, my German Liberal Prayer Book, *Die Kritiken* by Immanuel Kant, and Leo Baeck's *Dieses Volk – Jüdische Existenz (This People – Jewish Existence).*

It was a dull, autumn day. I went with my suitcase to the Berlin-Charlottenburg railway station and looked for an American Army officer who was waiting to take me along on a troop train leaving Berlin for Frankfurt. He made me board the train and he gave strict instructions to me to hide under his greatcoat in the railway compartment. Russian soldiers were not allowed to board the train, but they could look through the windows and order civilians off it. At last the train started to move and I could come out of my hiding place from under his coat.

The ruins of the city slid past and a great sadness overcame me, as I suddenly realised the full significance of this moment. I was about to leave behind my German Jewish history, my parents, who still lived in the Russian Zone of Germany, my mother tongue, the concerts and the theatre I loved to frequent, my medical career, and my many Jewish and German friends with whom I had shared the dark hours in Europe during its recent history.

I also realised that my ability to read Shakespeare at school in English classes did little to help me to understand the English conversation that took place all around me in this train. This was not a very solid foundation for settling in Australia and for making a living in in this country.

The journey continued from Frankfurt to Paris. I arrived in Paris at the Gare de L'Est after a long and strenuous journey, having to sit up in the third-class railway compartment for hours. It was very early morning, and an ill-tempered official of HIAS greeted me. "Do you need a hotel room? Do you need money to live?" he asked me. He was surprised, in fact I think he did not believe me when I told him that all I owned were a few East German marks, which had no value whatsoever outside East Germany. "I thought you guys earned on the black market in Berlin lots of *Lokshen* [American dollars]. You must sign for the money you receive from HIAS and as soon as you start to earn money in Australia, we expect you to repay us. Do you understand?" he said.

I understood, I signed, and I repaid it all in due course. Fully realising the difficulties ahead of me, I asked for the minimum amount I needed to live on. I used most of this money to visit museums and places of history in Paris and I put myself on a starvation diet. I was used to being hungry from my years in the camps and could catch up with eating in Australia. He led me to a small hotel in the Rue Jarry, a short street with down-market hotels, frequented by prostitutes. The asset value of these hotels depended on the number of *chambres pour la nuit* let per hour. "Room for the night" was a euphemism, as most of the hotel rooms were not let for the whole night, but just for as long as it took to have sex with the hired woman.

The few Jewish migrants in transit were very welcome by the owners of these hotels. Their rather lengthy stay in a room legitimised the hotel's existence. Everyone else checking in got a key to the room and a small towel. I got a key only, as I did not check in with a partner to have sex, so I was not entitled to the towel for a quick clean up after the event. "Don't get tangled up with these women," the HIAS man said when he left me.

I was soon to be investigated by my fellow Jews living in the same and in adjoining hotels, but they found me of little interest. I was a *Yekke* (German Jew), did not speak Yiddish too well and I wasted my time in museums learning about the history of this city, instead of making a quick buck here and there. I was to sink even lower in their eyes when they asked me one morning why I was a little better dressed than usual and where I was going. I replied, "I'm off to the synagogue for the Day of Atonement service."

"He's not just a *Yekke,* but also a *meschuggener* (crazy person)," I overheard one saying to the other.

The word *Yekke* is often interpreted as "German Jew" because Polish Jews believed that German Jews wear jackets and not a kaftan as some Polish Jews wore. However, *Yekke* is more likely an acronym for the Hebrew *Yehudi Kashe Havana* (A stupid Jew).

Our relationship was soon to change. The lack of food and the exhaustion from walking the length and breadth of Paris caught up with me. I was laid up with influenza. Suddenly, my coreligionists showed me their warmth and kindness. They called a doctor and brought gallons of chicken broth to restore me back to health.

One day, one of the men, when bringing the chicken soup, was crying like a little child. He asked me in a state of agitation: "Have you heard that the princess is dead?" Who was the princess? She was a young, good-looking prostitute who stood out from all the other old professionals. She never had to look for clients in the street for long. He told me the princess had jumped out of the window of the hotel and broken her neck when hitting the pavement. He was waiting in Paris to emigrate to Argentina and had left his young wife and child behind in

Poland to follow him later. "You know," he said, "I love my wife and child, but you need a woman, and the princess was great." He had just slept with the princess and had to see what was happening in the street. He left me behind to drink the chicken soup and to think and ponder. Would he ever get around to migrating to Argentina? What chance was there for his family to follow him? How long would it be before he found himself another princess from the army of prostitutes in Paris to brighten up his leisure hours between making money on the black market? Was he just weak and kind but enjoying life, in contrast to me, who was at the time just a bystander and an observer of the real world? The words of the prophet Amos came to mind: "I have set before you good and evil; choose." Maybe Amos did choose without thinking, but I was mostly thinking without getting on with making choices.

On my first outing, after being confined to bed for some days, I noticed that the man at the reception desk, who always handed out the room keys and the little white towels to the prostitutes and their clients, had gone, and another man had taken his place. On enquiring, I found out that the regular concierge was the owner of the Hotel Savoy, who had gone on holidays to his villa in Mentone, to recover from the upset caused to all parties with a financial interest in the Rue Jarry by the untimely death of the princess. He owned a luxury car which he parked a few streets away from his hotel. It was so good to learn that some people are most sensitive and do watch their etiquette!

The Dog

"Forgiveness is the key to action and freedom." – Hannah Arendt (1906-75)

The real purpose of my sojourn in Paris was to get a passage on a liner from Marseille or Genoa to Australia, but there was little I could do about hastening this process. I just had to wait patiently for my turn to be allocated a passage on an ocean liner. Meanwhile, my time was filled in with learning French, visiting castles, churches and museums and viewing from park benches and during my walks along almost every street of this beautiful city, the life of luxury and elegance, as well as the existence of abject poverty and despair. After the crowds in the camps and the comradeship of Berlin University life, I was alone among millions of people who made up the life of this city.

I visited the great cemeteries of Paris to stop and reflect on the lives of some who had struggled in bygone days to find meaning and purpose in a life in exile. In the Cimetière de Montmartre, I found the grave of Heinrich Heine (1797-1856), the great German lyrical poet and writer whose books Hitler burned, but whose poem the "Lorelei" was so much part of the German cultural heritage, that Hitler had to leave it in the school books and give Heine the greatest compliment any poet could ever receive, by stating its source as "German folk song – poet unknown." Almost one hundred years before it all happened in the Third Reich, Heine wrote: "First they burn books and then they burn people." He was baptised, but he explained to his friends: "The certificate of baptism is merely an entrance ticket into European culture." This entrance ticket was of limited duration. The hatred of the Jewish religion turned into a hatred of the Jewish people in the twentieth century.

Before Heine died, he was asked his thoughts about his adopted faith. He replied: "After all the Church has taught about the Jews, it is no longer possible for a Jew to believe in the divinity of another Jew." His grave was covered with a wreath from the city of Düsseldorf, the place of his birth, and his gravestone had survived the Nazi occupation of Paris. A walk in this cemetery was like taking a lesson in European cultural history, as one passed the graves of the writers and composers of bygone days. Autumn had transformed the old trees into a fairyland of colour.

Most evenings, weather permitting, I walked in Paris from my little hotel near the Gare de L'Est to the Champs-Élysées, and sat on a bench near one of the great fountains watching the world go by. Coming from the ruins of Berlin, one could live in the illusion that time had stood still and nothing had ever happened to disturb the peace in Europe.

One day, a middle-aged, kindly looking man joined me. He had with him a cute little dog on a leash. The dog took an instant liking to me and I took to the dog. It seemed to give the man great pleasure to see that his pet dog was suitably acknowledged. He started to chat to me. He noticed my accent, and asked me in perfect

German: *"Sind Sie Deutscher?"* (Are you a German?) I simply replied *"Ja",* as I thought it inappropriate to tell a stranger my whole life's history. He exploded with rage. He got up and told me that he was a Jew and that my kind and I had murdered his parents. He spat into my face, dragged the dog along with him and disappeared into the crowd. I was stunned, wiped his spit off my face and felt nauseated.

The beautiful city around me faded into the background on my way home to the hotel. I could not sleep that night. I had to learn with great sadness that the Holocaust had taught some Jews how to hate.

The Jewish Festival of Shavuot (Weeks) is also called *Seman Matan Torahtenu* (The time of the giving of the Law). Rabbinic commentary states that the Torah was "given" to all Jews, but "received and understood" by only a few. The man who spat into my face appeared to be a Jew by birth, tradition and in accordance with the Nuremberg Laws, but the teaching of Judaism had not reached his soul.

I attended the Day of Atonement service in the great Rue de la Victoire synagogue a few days later. There he was. We left the synagogue after the long day of prayer and reflection. Our eyes met. You could see, expressed upon his face, the realisation of what he had done. He waved to me and tried to reach me through the crowd. I pressed on and took shelter in the darkness of the night. He wanted to find peace of mind by merely apologising to a fellow Jew. He had come to the realisation that the "Germans" are just like the "Jews", a group of individuals who can be compassionate as well as hate. To both Germans and Jews, a new generation will be born beyond good and evil. Both their descendants will again have to learn the lesson of the Torah: "Love your neighbour because he is like you are". But the survivors of the Holocaust will no longer be alive and able to teach that there is no place for hate in civilised society. There will not be a physical survival without an ethical survival.

My frequent visits to the Latin Quarter with its Sorbonne University aroused nostalgia and self-examination within me. Would I be able to continue my medical studies in Australia or had the move from Berlin irrevocably ended these plans for my future life? Some 1700 years earlier, Jewish hopes were dashed in this place. There the Romans founded the city of Luteatia, which much later was renamed Paris. Here once stood Roman temples, residences, theatre, and the Imperial Palace. Nothing of it is left except part of the Thermae of the palace, which is now part of the Cluny Museum. In this palace lived for some time the Roman Emperor Flavius Claudius Julianus (331-363 CE), nicknamed Julian the Apostate. He revoked the Jew Tax, and promised to rebuild the Temple in Jerusalem under the supervision of the scholar Alpius of Antiochia. The Jews at the time had their dreams destroyed when Julian died in the battle of Ktesipon. How often can one survive the vicissitudes of life and rebuild a future on the shaky foundations of the past?

I started to realise that after twelve years trying to escape from Hitler's Germany, I had been programmed to think that emigration was my destiny. My stay in Paris made me question anew whether emigration was my only option. Was my life not deeply rooted in the history of European Jewry? The problem I had to confront was that my world had become the world of yesterday. All that was dear to me had lost its reality; it was now nothing but a memory.

On my return to the hotel I found a letter from the Paris HIAS office on my bed, asking me to see them urgently. The die was cast. They had managed to get me on a boat to Australia.

Terra Australis

"When all else is lost, the future still remains." – Christian Nestell Bovee (1820-1904)

The entrance ticket to my future life in Australia was given to me in the Paris office of HIAS. It was a dormitory-class ticket for the Italian liner *Surriento* to sail from Genoa on 31 October 1949 and to arrive in Fremantle, Western Australia on 26 November. I was given just a few hours' notice, to pack up and vacate my Paris hotel room.

The train journey from the Gare de Lyon to Genoa opened for me a new vista on the world. Southern France and northern Italy passed by the window of the slow train. Later, seeing Genoa, Naples, Malta, Port Said, Aden and Colombo for the first time opened another window on a New World, so different from the medieval city of Breslau that had been my entire world for so many years.

The *Surriento* was dirty and smelly, and I shared a small dormitory with eight people in the bowels of this 35,000-ton liner. Some refugees from Italy and Eastern Europe had managed to persuade the boarding staff to allow them to take more than the permitted amount of cabin luggage into the dormitory and this made it almost impossible to move about. A few passengers must have been told that the quality of meals on board ship was poor and so they travelled with lots of bread, salami, sausages, and all kinds of other food items. I had to struggle with the ship's staple diet of spaghetti Bolognese, pickled olives and vegetables, while my cabin mates gorged themselves with their BYO food. The boat was overcrowded, and there were lots of people, especially screaming children, everywhere.

In every port, most passengers booked to go on interesting tours. I had no money to spend, and so I missed seeing the ruins of Pompeii, the bazaars of Port Said, and the many other tourist attractions on the way. But when walking on my own through the streets of Genoa, Naples, Colombo and Palermo, I saw faces reflecting extreme poverty, despair and anger. During the 26 days of my journey to Australia, I could observe the full spectrum of the human condition, from the luxury and wealth of the Champs-Élysées in Paris to the dire poverty in the slums of Palermo. It became obvious that we were heading into a troubled world, in which the underprivileged would no longer be kept at bay with the prayers and pious promises of world religions. No doubt the time was going to come when all these problems would also catch up with the "lucky country", Australia.

At last the faint outline of the *"Australia del Espiritu Santo"* (The Southern Land of the Holy Spirit), as the Portuguese explorer Pedro Fernandez de Quiros called this continent, appeared. I stood at the railing of the boat and strained my eyes trying to see what I would encounter when I set foot on land.

Going down the gangplank, I saw a man with a red carnation in his lapel. This would be my father's cousin Erich Schimmelburg-Shilbury, who was waiting for me and wearing the carnation as we had arranged by letter. The last time we had met was twelve years ago, in Berlin in 1937, when I was merely nine years old. Erich took me into his family with great warmth and affection and we discovered that we had a lot in common. A friend of Erich, who was the proud owner of a car and offered to drive us home, accompanied him.

On the way, we drove through the Australian bush, and stopped in Kings Park to look down on the city of Perth and the Swan River. At that time, Western Australia had only 350,000 inhabitants, of whom 300,000 lived in its capital, Perth, and the remaining 50,000 lived in the rest of this vast state. It was not foreseeable that in the next 50 years Perth would grow to a population of over two million.

I had to learn many hard lessons in the first two weeks in Western Australia. They were: my ability to speak English was inadequate, and communications were ineffective. My German *Abitur* (Tertiary Entrance Examination) was not recognised, nor was the Western Australian University prepared to give me any credit for subjects I had successfully passed at Berlin University.

My knowledge of Russian, Greek, Latin, German and French and my interest in art, music and science were little appreciated in this Anglo-Celtic society. Indeed, it set me apart from the Aussies, and made me feel like a polar bear in the Sahara Desert.

My fellow Jews had a greater interest in the latest cricket and football scores than in the Holocaust, and to most of them I was a *Yekke* who, they believed, would not know much about Jewish matters. The only contribution of the local Jewish community to my plight was to present me almost instantly with the account for my sea-voyage to Australia and the cost of my stay in Paris, coupled with an urgent request to settle this account at the very earliest.

I arrived in Perth about four months before my twenty-first birthday and four weeks before Christmas. The former fact was a great handicap, as employers were not interested in an unskilled worker whose wage had to be increased from a junior rate to a senior rate within four months. The latter fact gave me a lucky break. A job as an assistant postman came my way. It was hot, I worked for little pay, and all the dogs in the streets in which I delivered letters appeared at first rather ferocious. It did not take long to make friends with the dogs and the people too became friendly as time went along. I could start to repay my debt, and start my new life beyond survival as an unskilled foreign Jew in a Christian British country.

Those who arrived in this continent thousands of years before I did, loved this country's harsh beauty. They became self-reliant in its solitude, and found meaning in the life of their "Dreamtime." It was Martin Buber who wrote: "The present is the eclipse between the past and the future." For me, the past was a rich tapestry of human experience. The future in Australia was no less challenging, and it has remained so. Since surviving the Holocaust, every moment of my life has been an eclipse of so much of the past for which to be grateful, and so much of the future to work for with all my remaining strength.

Ken and Judith Arkwright after Ken received the Order of Australia at Government House in Western Australia.

Unity or Diversity?

"There is a history in all men's lives." – William Shakespeare *(Henry IV)*

Aristotle (384-322 BCE) suggested that literature should have:

1) unity of action;
2) unity of time; and
3) unity of place.

In contrast, Johann Wolfgang von Goethe (1749-1832) advises a writer in the prelude to his masterpiece the play *Faust:*

You can compel the mass by mass alone;
Each in the end will seek out something as his own.
Bring much and you'll bring this or that to everyone
And each will leave contented when the play is done.
If you will give a piece, give it at once in pieces!
Ragout like this your fame increases.

I have tried to stick to the advice of Aristotle, but family and friends keep on asking me to tell some family gossip and scandals, just like Goethe tells them about the life of *Faust* in two very long plays.

My grandfather's uncle Hermann Aufrichtig (1828-1900) lived in Breslau-Silesia and initially made his living as a peddler. He persuaded my grandfather Isidor Aufrichtig (1856-1934) to establish with him a ladies overcoat factory called H. Aufrichtig, that was financially so successful that my grandfather retired and allowed his uncle's growing family to continue to develop this business. Isidor was self-educated and had a large library of classical Greek and Latin writers and philosophers. He read them all in Greek and Latin and not in translation.

Grandfather married Emma (née Schimmelburg) Aufrichtig (1862-1938) and they had four boys together. Three boys died at or after birth, and my father Rudolf Aufrichtig/Arkwright (1893-1978) was the only long-term survivor. In 1928 he married my mother Frieda (née Schneider) Aufrichtig.

Father joined an international grain trading business in 1912 but had to leave it to serve in the German Army Infantry in WWI (1914-18). He served on the Eastern and Western fronts, was wounded three times and was decorated with the Iron Cross. He served the German government in 1919 and 1920 to control the supply and distribution of grain. In 1921 he founded with a friend a luxury ladies shoe factory in Berlin called Basch und Aufrichtig, which he merged with a Germany-wide shoe manufacturing and retailing business.

On 31 March 1934 the business was Aryanised, his bank account was closed and he was subjected to forced labour. We had to move from one *Judenhaus* to another, living in just one room, and this journey ended up in labour and concentration camps and finally living under a false name in early 1944-45.

My relationship with my father and mother was more than just one of parents and son – it was also a close friendship. However, this is not obvious from my story as told in previous chapters of this book.

I was supposed to have been deported to the labour camp together with my father, but I was diagnosed with scarlet fever and associated heart complications. Consequently, I was put into the Jewish hospital. The Jewish hospital at that time was located inside the small administration building in the Cosel Jewish Cemetery. The diagnosis of scarlet fever had the advantage that the visiting Gestapo officers would not check on it, out of fear of infection. The associated heart condition diagnosis would delay my deportation to the labour camp. I understand that Jewish women at that time were often put into this hospital for pregnancy termination, as a pregnant Jewish woman risked immediate deportation to prevent another Jew from being born.

This idea of hospitalisation for protection from persecution was not entirely new. In 1938, *Kristallnacht,* the then director of the large 350-bed Breslau Jewish hospital, Dr Ludwig Guttmann, instructed the staff of that hospital to admit without question any

Jew who was in danger of being deported to the Buchenwald concentration camp. Ludwig Guttmann was the founder of the Paralympic Games and his son Dieter (Dennis) Guttmann was a schoolmate of mine.

The scarlet fever did have one other negative effect. My father and I ended up in different barracks in the labour camp, because we arrived in there at different times. Therefore, we had little contact with each other.

When we later escaped from concentration camp and lived underground, we acted as unrelated strangers, otherwise if one of us had been discovered by the Gestapo, son and father would automatically be killed together. By pretending to be strangers, there was at least a slight chance of one of us surviving, should the other be caught.

I left my mother for the labour and KZ camps when I was thirteen years old. We had a normal loving mother-son relationship until then. Two years later when I returned to Breslau, my mother had done two years of slave labour in the FAMO *(Fahrzeug- und Motorenwerke,* auto and engine works), a German vehicle manufacturer that at the time was producing military vehicles.

She had been loaded onto a boat with the remaining Breslau Jews and the boat was to be blown up in the middle of the Oder River. A Russian artillery attack saved the day and made it necessary for the Gestapo to postpone this operation. She then hid in the cellars of bombed-out houses, eating whatever stored food she could find. She stayed in Breslau, which was then transformed into the Polish City of Wrocław, hoping that we might still be alive.

She never talked about these experiences. However, they affected her mental wellbeing before she died. She would lock herself in her home and point to people in the street below, claiming they were coming to get her for deportation.

When I left, we were mother and child; when I returned, mother and I were hated Germans and Jews in the eyes of the new Polish citizens of the city of Wrocław. It took time to adjust and to learn about our new status in life, and to leave Wrocław and start a new life in the city of Erfurt in the American Zone of Germany on 12 September 1945. Just a short time after we had settled there, it was given by the Western Allies to the Russian Zone of Germany in exchange for the Russian Zone of Germany allowing an American, French and British Zone to be created in Berlin.

My parents lived in Erfurt until 21 October 1950. My father became receiver-manager of a large shoe factory, followed by creating an exchange warehouse business and becoming its director, and finally being appointed director for economic planning for the East German province of Thuringia.

The East German government told my parents that they were required to host in their home in Erfurt, East German spies who came to East Germany from the West to report their findings. My parents refused to comply, without success. So they acquired a ferocious Alsatian dog called Axel, hoping this would make the visitors uncomfortable. This did not work. The commanding officer asked my parents to leave their home so the spy conference could take place, and return later.

This government decision made my parents flee East Germany and live in West Berlin until I was able to help them to immigrate to Australia. Once again I had to learn how to communicate with them without endangering their lives. I sent them letters signed with different names and posted from different places, always written on different typewriters, hoping that they would understand the true meaning behind the vague text of the letters.

And what did I do with my life? That is for another book, maybe some time in the future ... Now, just a few notes.

I did my normal German Leaving certificate by working day and night to catch up with the school education lost during the Hitler years. I studied medicine at Humboldt University in Berlin, but then left Germany for Australia, due to political pressure put upon me in East Germany. Australia did not like 'bloody foreigners' at that time.

I arrived in Fremantle on 26 November 1949 and consequently all my achievements in Germany were of no value in Australia. Back to the slog! The result was an Associate Commerce degree from Perth Technical College and FCPA, FAICA, FAICD and FRMIA.

I worked in the steel industry, metal manufacturing and the retail industry as an accountant, cost accountant, manager and director. I participated in management positions in the Retail Traders Associations of WA, the Chamber of Commerce and Industry of WA and the WA government at the Asian Productivity Forum in Tokyo.

It was not all business! I translated a collection of three volumes of German poems into English to be published by Academic Press International and my book *Jenseits des Überlebens* was published by the *Stiftung Denkmal fűr die ermordeten Juden Europas,* Uwe Neumärker und Katherina Friedla in 2011.

There is a saying in the Talmud: "Only man and woman together constitute a human being."

I studied music, violin and singing at the Conservatorium in Erfurt. I enjoyed making music again in Australia in orchestras and string quartets, playing the violin, and especially classical Jewish synagogue music. I met Marian Masel who sang regularly art song at the ABC and her husband Philip Masel who at the end of his life was an ABC commissioner.

They had a charming, beautiful, bright and kind daughter Judith who reminded me of the Talmudic wisdom that Judith and I together could perhaps constitute a complete human being. It was the best decision of my life! In addition, we had two sons and four grandchildren. You want to know more about it? Then you must wait for my next book!

(l-r) Peter, Judith, Kevin and Ken Arkwright.

Epilogue

"I can promise to be honest but I cannot promise to be unbiased."
– Johann Wolfgang von Goethe (1749-1832)

In the beginning, it was believed that history is the record of God's intervention in the lives of men. Later, ruthless rulers forced historians to write history so that it would show these rulers in the most favourable light. Historians had to describe the actions of selfish dictators, their evil deeds and selfish ambitions as God-inspired. Adolf Hitler spoke about the *Göttliche Vorsehung* (Divine Providence) that made him survive all 40 attempts on his life, and that made it his destiny to lead Germany to achieve "the fulfilment of its mission in history."

In contrast, the Roman historian Publius Cornelius Tacitus (56-117 CE) demanded that history should be written *sine ira et studio* (objectively). This also proved to be an elusive ideal.

The Jewish reason for writing history is to remember the successes and failures in human endeavour, and to learn from the lessons of history. I have tried to give you a little insight into what I have seen, and acquaint you with some of the people I have met on my 88-year journey through life.

My experiences have taught me that to rely upon the struggle within one's self to achieve ethical action, is more likely to succeed than to hope for supernatural salvation from outside. I fully acknowledge that this Jewish view of the world is not the only valid interpretation. I fail to understand how churches could have found "Communion with God" by sharing a cup of wine representing the blood of the Jew Jesus, when at the same time they turned their back on the blood of six million Jews being spilled.

I am deeply concerned that, after the Holocaust, far too much has been written by and about the Jewish people that deals merely with physical survival and national rebuilding. I firmly believe that Jewish survival is not about getting lost in never-ending grief, nor is it about excessive national pride. Survival is about every human being finding meaning in his or her own actions and lives. The tragedy of the Holocaust is not encapsulated in the photos of burning synagogues and the bulldozing of dead bodies into a pit; not in the ruins of defunct crematoria and gas chambers, but in the suffering and destruction of every single human life. The lesson of the Holocaust is not contained in the total of six million lost Jewish lives, but it speaks to us through the suffering of every individual soul lost, multiplied by six million.

Presently, the world is troubled by religious fundamentalists who claim to be in possession of the truth. The German poet Gotthold Ephraim Lessing (1729-81) wrote: "Dear God, if you would have the whole truth in your right hand, and the eternal striving for truth in your left hand, and if you would say to me, choose, I would ask You to give me your left hand, as the whole truth is denied to us and reserved for You alone." The Jewish world is not free from this human failing. Ultra-Orthodox Jewish fundamentalists claim to be in possession of the truth, and in their arrogance, they often defile the wisdom and teaching of Judaism and drown out the still, quiet voice of humanity and truth.

A man once posed a question to a chess master. "What is the best move in the world in a game of chess?" The answer given was: "There is no best move, not even a good move that can be defined apart from a particular situation in a game, and apart from the particular persona of one's opponent." Likewise, in the game of living, I have never found a best way to act or the truest meaning of life. Every man's task is unique, every moment of man's life is unique and requires its own response.

I would like to thank my publisher Hybrid Publishers for their expertise and attention to detail and especially to Louis de Vries and Anna Rosner Blay.

Somerset Maugham wrote: "All the words I use in my stories can be found in the dictionary – it's just a matter of arranging them into the right sentences."

Louis and Anna drew attention to my failure to take Somerset Maugham's advice at times, which I believe does make this book better than it would have otherwise been.

In conclusion, I need to express my deep gratitude for great gifts life has allotted to me. I wish to acknowledge my wife Judith's contribution to this book with typing and research, but more importantly, by correcting the deficiencies in my persona and thereby making this account more balanced. She is without doubt my "better half".

Raising children means to make them be independent in thought and action. They need to live their own lives, and should not be encouraged to relive ours. And yet we always hope that the generation to follow us will continue with the good of the past, and will not repeat our mistakes. So, I hope that our sons Peter and Kevin, and their families, as they read this book, will review our lives as Jews, Germans, Europeans and Australians, and finally, as members of the family of man.

The writer Ernst Toller (1893-1939) wrote at the end of his life: "Jewish parents have given me life; Germany has educated me; Europe is my fatherland; the world is my home." I can identify with these sentiments, but I need to add that Australia has a special place in my heart for making me appreciate the vastness and beauty of the world in which we live. A New York rabbi once sent a telegram to Albert Einstein in Princeton, asking whether Einstein believed in God. Einstein replied: "I believe in the God of Baruch Spinoza, who reveals himself in the orderly harmony of everything that exists, but not in a God who looks after the fate and the actions of man." The last sentence in Baruch Spinoza's book *Ethics* is: *Sed omnia praeclara tam difficilia quam rara sunt.* (Everything that is very clear and great, is as difficult to realise as it is rare.)

To merely have survived is without meaning, unless we pursue the many opportunities and challenges life does offer, even **beyond survival.**

www.ingramcontent.com/pod-product-compliance
Lightning Source LLC
LaVergne TN
LVHW010538100826
845148LV00001B/221

9780369355133